He Loved and Served
The Story of Curtis Kelsey

Dr. H. Motamed
35 Wensley Dr.
Great Neck, NY 11021

He Loved and Served

The Story of Curtis Kelsey

by

NATHAN RUTSTEIN

GEORGE RONALD
OXFORD

GEORGE RONALD, Publisher
46 High Street, Kidlington, Oxford OX5 2DN

ISBN 0-85398-120-5 (cloth)
ISBN 0-85398-121-3 (paper)

Printed in the United States of America

NOTE TO THE READER

Quotations from Bahá'í Scripture in this book have been carefully checked for accuracy; every effort has also been made to ensure the authenticity of factual accounts and details. However, many of the conversations related are based on the notes of those present, or on tape recordings made of the participants recalling them from memory, and have not necessarily been reproduced verbatim. Inevitably, the majority of notes and recordings come from Curtis Kelsey himself, and a number of brief remarks attributed to 'Abdu'l-Bahá are therefore of the nature of Pilgrims' Notes. This means that they do not have the same authority as Bahá'í Holy Text.

Chapter 1

It was a small room, plain, with an iron post bed and a narrow mattress, and a simple chest of drawers with a pitcher of water on top. The early autumn sun streamed into the room, which was wrapped in silence, despite the presence of two men inside. 'Abdu'l-Bahá was in the far corner gazing into the eyes of a young American sitting on a chair, holding a cup of tea which he never drew to his lips.

The Master had asked for Curtis Kelsey to come to His room. Wondering why he had been summoned, Curtis had entered, concerned that perhaps he had done something wrong. But the work he had been asked to do seemed to be progressing smoothly, and he hadn't alienated anyone, as far as he knew.

'Abdu'l-Bahá never uttered a word, just stared at the young man, who had come from halfway around the world. Curtis couldn't say anything, but not because the Master adhered to some special protocol. In fact, there had been many times when Curtis initiated conversation with the Master.

But inside 'Abdu'l-Bahá's room that day in 1921, Curtis didn't wish to say anything, though at first he wondered why he had been asked to be alone with the Master.

Meeting 'Abdu'l-Bahá's gaze seemed too much to endure. At first Curtis wanted to look at the walls, or outside at the sun-parched grounds; but he couldn't. 'Abdu'l-Bahá's gaze was a divine command – and Curtis obeyed.

In his heart, Curtis knew 'Abdu'l-Bahá wasn't reprimanding him. He believed there had to be a reason for what was happening at that moment.

Soon his uneasiness vanished, giving way to serenity. Curtis had surrendered; all his reserve had evaporated; stripped of every selfish thought, his reality was utterly exposed to eyes reflecting power beyond human dimension. He couldn't turn away from the Master. There was nothing in that room but 'Abdu'l-Bahá. The Master had swept the lanky, Utah-born young man into a different world, a world of love, of joy. For the first time in his life he had been embraced by ecstasy. He would have stayed in that room forever, because time ceased to have meaning; nothing else mattered but being the recipient of the love flowing from 'Abdu'l-Bahá. Finally, the Master smiled – and said that Curtis could leave.

Only years later did Curtis begin to understand the significance of that spiritual journey he experienced with 'Abdu'l-Bahá. Whenever he was beset with serious problems, 'Abdu'l-Bahá's face would come to mind, generating courage, confidence, the will to solve what appeared insoluble. Other things would happen, which some people might consider miracles, but which Curtis felt were 'the bounties of God, something everyone could experience.'

Chapter 2

Curtis Kelsey was a simple man, who never gained worldly fame. In a formal sense, he was poorly educated, never progressing beyond the eighth grade. It wasn't because his parents didn't care. They urged him, especially his father, to go on to college, sending him to different kinds of school, hoping there would be one he would like; but there wasn't a school that could hold him. Various public and private schools were tried, including a military academy. His most fruitful experience was at a trade school, where he was able to build things, some of which were so good they were exhibited at the Seattle World's Fair. But the trade school experience was short-lived. Classroom learning was a bore, and when a teacher told him that he resembled a duck-billed platypus, he vowed never to return to school. Life was going to be his teacher.

Those who knew Curtis superficially in the early 1900s probably thought he was a rebel. Adventurous, he sought new experiences and found pleasure in making things that did something useful. That was something he rarely experienced in school. In a sense he was a frontiersman, continually exploring, open to new ideas. Perhaps he came by his frontier spirit naturally. His father's ancestors fought against the British in the Revolutionary War with Ethan Allen's Green Mountain Boys and after the war pioneered to the Kentucky wilderness. Curtis' mother's ancestors left the east to farm in Kansas.

Curtis was born in 1894 in Salt Lake City, Utah, where his father designed the city's first water works. The Rocky Mountains fascinated him; he loved the open spaces, the touch of the soil; he loved to roam, unrestricted. As a child he enjoyed the times when his father's close friend William Cody (Buffalo Bill) would visit the family, telling stories of the Old West, handing Curtis and his three brothers silver dollar coins, and tickets to his Wild West circus show.

Curtis was a westerner, always was, even when he worked in New York City. He was an open person – pure-hearted, some would say. His laughter was free-flowing, whole-hearted and often accompanied with a slap of his knee. He never gave up hope of returning to the west one day to work a ranch.

Curtis didn't grow up in a traditionally religious home. His father Frank, a Lincolnesque figure, an engineer who helped to develop many of the irrigation and power systems in the western United States, had little patience for organized religion. He was a man of sterling integrity, who couldn't abide underhandedness and scheming. He quit his job as Salt Lake City's city engineer rather than deal with the corrupt politicians who were in power. Not even appeals from Mormon Church officials, who admired his character and professional ability, were able to change Frank Kelsey's decision. For a while he remained in Salt Lake City, operating an engineering firm with Brigham Young's youngest son. Curtis' father never embraced Mormonism, despite considerable pressure from church leaders and relatives who had been converted.

The disunity among the Christians soured Frank Kelsey to church-going. He was a practical man who believed that all that mattered was being honest, 'living up to your ideals and making sure you do what you say you'll do.' Young Curtis was impressed with his father's philosophy, and the way he lived it. His admiration for Abraham Lincoln was undoubtedly due to his father's deep respect for America's sixteenth president, who believed in God but rejected organized religion. As a youth Curtis carried with him a number of sayings of Lincoln, which he would draw upon for inspiration during stressful times.

But it was his mother, Valeria, who had a more profound influence on him. She was a gentle soul who possessed great inner strength and was sensitive to the way men and women were expected to behave in the early 1900s. Though she never embarrassed the men closest to her, in her own way she was a fighter for women's rights, a free thinker, someone who continually searched for ways to improve the lot of all people. Valeria De Mude Kelsey had a way of getting her way, without bludgeoning anyone. Most people she dealt with, men and women, were dazzled by her sparkle and wit, her universal outlook, and her uncannily accurate intuition. Her depth of feeling and keen insight into human behavior earned her respect among all who had dealings with her.

A successful poet, her writing reflected a yearning for greater understanding between people, and a deep love for God.

Although reared in a fundamentalist Baptist family in Kansas, she found that kind of religion stifling as an adult. But unlike her husband, she felt their children needed some religious training, so she allowed them to choose whatever church they liked. When Curtis was old enough to make that kind of decision, the Kelsey family was living in Portland, Oregon. Mrs Kelsey was especially concerned that Curtis receive spiritual training, because he, more than her other children, appeared to her to have a greater spiritual capacity. It was something she knew when she held him in her arms as an infant and watched him play with other children. And it wasn't something that was easily noticed with the outer eye, because as a child he was strong-willed and independent-minded. But she followed her intuition and persisted in nourishing his spiritual nature, even when he reached adulthood and turned away from religion.

Curtis joined the Baptist Sunday School only because that church was the closest one to his home. But two months later he was going to another Protestant church, because a friend claimed that his minister was a 'regular guy,' who took the Sunday School on camping trips and gave Christmas gifts. While attending religious classes, he adhered to his mother's advice: 'Don't swallow all they tell you in Sunday School ... do your own thinking.' In his spare time, he looked into Christian Science, other Protestant sects, New Thought, Spiritualism; he even experimented with a Ouija Board and Table-Lifting.

His first and last encounter with Table-Lifting occurred at a friend's home in northern California. Curtis and five others were assembled in a totally dark room, sitting silently, with their fingers under a table, barely touching it, waiting for the spirits to come and lift it. In order to discourage her son from dabbling with the occult, the mother of Curtis' friend decided to disrupt the secret spiritual ritual. She tip-toed up the stairs, quietly opened her son's bedroom door – and screamed. The table went right up to the ceiling – but not because of souls in the spirit world. When she turned on the light, she found six young men sprawled on the floor in a state of shock.

After his Table-Lifting experience, Curtis heeded his father's advice to stop wasting his time looking into different religious beliefs.

Though not religious as a youth, Curtis had a deep appreciation for spiritual values – and practiced them, rarely deviating from them, despite his adventurous spirit and his passion for teasing and initiating pranks.

He couldn't abide hypocrites and those who practiced a double standard. A leading physician in town became aware of this dislike through an encounter with Curtis.

Not going to school and not knowing what career to pursue, Curtis seemed to be leading a chartless course in life when he turned eighteen. His father was disappointed in what he considered were Curtis' shiftless ways. This troubled Curtis; and when he evaluated his situation – the present seemed confusing and the future scared him – he would grow exceedingly tense and depressed.

Concerned about Curtis' emotional state, his parents had him examined by a family friend and leading neurologist. After listening to Curtis explain how he felt, the physician told Curtis that there was a very natural way of curing his ailment. 'Son,' he said, 'you should go out and find a girl and sow some wild oats.'

That infuriated Curtis, for here was a highly respected

citizen, a regular church-goer, advocating something that his religion forbids. Curtis knew the doctor's daughter, who was attractive; and he knew how close the doctor was to her. Looking the physician right in the eye, Curtis said, 'Why don't I start with your daughter?'

Mrs Kelsey knew her son had an inquiring mind, so she never stopped sharing new ideas and philosophies with him. Even when he balked, she never grew dismayed. One day she came home excited, wanting to tell Curtis about something absolutely wonderful, something she had always known was somewhere in the world but could never find. 'Have you heard of the Bahá'í Movement, son?' she asked Curtis.

'Mother, you know I'm not interested in religious ideas anymore,' he said, showing some annoyance.

Mrs Kelsey became a Bahá'í in 1909, but though she didn't press her Faith on Curtis, she waited for the right time to mention it again. And that happened several months later when they were living in Tacoma, Washington. Roy Wilhelm, a Wall Street financier and coffee magnate, who acted as 'Abdu'l-Bahá's chief representative in the Western Hemisphere, was to speak about the Bahá'í Movement at the Kelsey home. Several family friends were invited.

Despite Curtis' reluctance to delve into anything religious, Mrs Kelsey approached him, urging him to stay home to meet Mr Wilhelm. Curtis wanted to play pool that night, not only because he enjoyed the game, but because it was a source of earning some spending money. He was one of the best players in Tacoma.

Mrs Kelsey got her way, but not entirely. Curtis remained home – in his woodshop in the basement. When he overheard his mother telling Mr Wilhelm that she wanted him to explain the Bahá'í Movement to her son, Curtis realized that there was no way of escaping, because the only way out of the woodshop was the way you entered it, through the kitchen, where his mother and Mr Wilhelm were talking. So he fortified himself for an evangelistic harangue. But Curtis didn't get what he anticipated. Mr Wilhelm never mentioned the Bahá'í Movement, not even God. Instead they talked about woodworking. Curtis was impressed by Mr Wilhelm's sincerity and his genuine interest in him as a person. 'He's not all cracked up about religion,' Curtis thought. 'He's a regular guy.'

After watching the young man demonstrate his turning lathe, Mr Wilhelm asked if Curtis would come east to help him set up a shop in his New Jersey home. When Curtis pointed out that he had no plans to go east, Mr Wilhelm responded, 'Well, you never know about these things; strange things happen.'

It was a strange statement to make, Curtis thought. For him, going to New Jersey would be like going to China. It was 3,000 miles away; he didn't know anyone there. He was rooted in the west and loved it. Curtis soon forgot what Mr Wilhelm told him.

Three months later Curtis was lured by the Ford adventure in Detroit. Mr Henry Ford was paying automobile workers five dollars a day making 'the average man's car.' No other manufacturing unit in the country was paying so high a wage. Many industrial tycoons and economists of the day felt Ford's pay scale was outrageous, that it was inflationary and would wreck the economy. Thousands of men streamed into Detroit, trying to get on the Ford Motor Company's payroll. Curtis' gamble proved fruitful: Ford hired him.

He enjoyed working on the Ford, but Detroit wasn't the west. There were no mountains, and the sky wasn't as clear. People weren't as friendly. Though impressed by the energy of the city, he longed for the openness of the westerners, their genuine willingness to help you when you needed help. Developing friendships was difficult because most of the workers had families. In order to overcome his loneliness, Curtis joined the Unitarian church. He chose that church because he knew the Unitarians were broad-minded, that no demands would be made on him, and you could believe whatever you wished to believe.

After the sermon one Sunday, the minister announced to the congregation that a distinguished gentleman from Persia would be speaking on the Bahá'í Faith immediately after the service.

'Strange,' Curtis thought, 'wherever I go I run into Bahá'í.' Only two people remained to hear Dr Díyá Baghdádí; and Curtis was one of them. The audience of two was looking at the minister and the black-haired, black-eyed gentleman dressed smartly in a black suit, white shirt and black tie. There was a special bearing about the Persian, Curtis felt.

After his introduction, the minister left, claiming he had another appointment. It was an odd situation: a beaming gentleman from the orient, standing before a podium, peering into the large hall, with row after row of empty pews. The fact that there were only two people in the audience didn't upset Dr Baghdádí. He spoke with deep feeling, with an enthusiasm that great orators display when speaking to huge crowds. It was a stirring talk, but Curtis couldn't remember what was said. All he could think about was why he was encountering the Bahá'í message again.

Curtis moved farther east – to New York. But it wasn't something he had planned. His family had moved to New York City, where his father organized the Continental Pipe Company, which designed and constructed pipelines for power and chemical companies.

One day Curtis received a letter from his father, asking him to visit the family during the Christmas period. A date for the trip was set, but a problem arose. The day before Curtis was to leave, his foreman, for some inexplicable reason, said he had to postpone his trip. When Curtis insisted that he was going, the foreman tried to physically block the way to the exit, warning him that he shouldn't abuse a job that paid him five dollars a day, something he couldn't earn anywhere else. Angered, Curtis said he was not only going to New York, but that he was quitting. That pronouncement frightened the foreman, because the company held its foremen accountable if any of their workers left the job. The Ford Motor Company found it difficult to understand why anyone would leave the working man's paradise that it had created. After all, no other company was paying so much money to its assembly workers, nor cared for them the way Mr Ford did.

New York City was unlike any other place Curtis had been to. There were so many different kinds of people, often speaking foreign languages or fractured English. In some parts of the city there were strange smells, wafting from the open windows of tenement houses swollen with immigrants from Eastern Europe. There wasn't a mountain anywhere to be seen, and the only animals he encountered were overworked horses, pulling wagons of ice, cans of milk, or hot loaves of rye and pumpernickel bread. Stray dogs and cats gathered around the meat-packing plants, competing for scraps. And there were so many people on the streets, all intent on getting somewhere quickly.

New York City was another world, fired by a commercial pioneering spirit. It was a place that seemed to foster ambition and inspire the daring and free-spirited to amass a fortune. Curtis wasn't immune to that spirit. Riding the elevator to his father's office on the thirty-ninth floor of the Woolworth Building, the tallest skyscraper in America in those days, was exciting. When his father offered him a job, Curtis couldn't refuse. And he was going to make more money than at Ford. But Curtis didn't ride the elevator much because he was made a field supervisor. His first assignment was to help manage the construction of a large wood pipeline for the General Electric Company, near Pittsfield, Massachusetts.

Curtis liked what he was doing, mainly because he was working outdoors. He knew that sitting behind a desk all day, even if it was on the thirty-ninth floor of the Woolworth Building, would be a bore. Besides, working in the Berkshire Mountains reminded him a little of the west; nothing as majestic and mighty as the Rockies, but being in the New England hills revived old, good feelings.

But Curtis didn't remain on the job long enough to see the pipeline completed. One day while in the woods, his head began to hurt. Probably just a headache, he thought, and continued to work. But the pain intensified; and after a night of restless sleep it didn't subside. His body began to ache and was seized by chills. For several days he worked, unable to drive off the pain. Finally he had to go home. The doctor who examined him said it was a good thing he didn't stay much longer in the Berkshires because he had contracted typhoid fever. About all he could do was wait the disease out – in bed. The headaches persisted. One night the ache and pounding were so severe that not even the ice pack his mother had given him could dull the pain. Frustrated, he buried his head in the pillow, crying for relief. Suddenly, the pain vanished, and the most wondrous music he had ever heard filled the room. Curtis turned, straining to see in the dark if people were around him playing instruments. But it was music that could only come from a great symphony orchestra. He lay back for a moment, being bathed by sounds so beautiful it didn't matter where they came from. His whole being had been penetrated by a magnificent feeling of well-being. He had to share this wonder with someone. He called his mother. As he began to sit up, the music began to fade.

When Mrs Kelsey entered the room, the music had disappeared. She turned the light on and found her son sitting up, relaxed, wonderment etched on his face.

'Mother,' he said, 'the strangest thing happened.'

'What was it?'

'I heard the most beautiful music.'

'Music?'

'Yes ... coming from some great orchestra.'

She moved closer to him, placing a hand on his forehead, thinking that perhaps his fever had driven him into delirium.

'No ... there's nothing wrong with me, mother,' he said.

'What about your headache?'

'When the music came it went away.'

Mrs Kelsey looked at her son for several seconds, then said, 'Maybe we can find the answer to your experience in the Bahá'í Writings.' She went to her room to fetch a book, pulled up a chair next to Curtis, and they started reading passages from Bahá'u'lláh. Curtis couldn't turn away from the book. 'Mother, why have you not told me about these Writings before?'

'I have tried for nine years,' she said, 'but you didn't show any interest.'

Mrs Kelsey turned to a passage and read it aloud: 'God screens us evermore from premature ideas ... our eyes cannot see things that stare us in the face until the hour arrives when the mind is ripened. Then we behold them, and the time when we saw them not is like a dream.' Curtis continued to read, then exclaimed, 'This is the truth!'

Curtis and his mother read some more. Though they didn't find what they were looking for, Curtis had discovered Bahá'u'lláh. When Mrs Kelsey returned to her room Curtis remained awake for a while, thinking about what had just transpired, and the thought of Roy Wilhelm came to mind – and the strange remark he had made that night in the wood-working shop in Tacoma, Washington.

When the doctor heard what had happened he couldn't believe it. He came the next day to examine Curtis and marveled at the way he had been cured.

Mrs Kelsey couldn't remember ever being happier. She contacted some of the Bahá'ís in New York City, asking them to come to her house, not only to see Curtis, but to help search through the Bahá'í Writings for at least a clue to her son's mysterious experience. Hooper Harris, Mary Hanford Ford, Howard Colby Ives, Mrs Florian Krug and others called on the Kelseys, bringing the few Bahá'í books they had, whatever Tablets they had from 'Abdu'l-Bahá, and any scraps of paper they had with Bahá'í Writings on them. In those days there wasn't much printed Bahá'í material. Usually, when a believer received a Tablet from the World Center, he would copy it out in longhand and share it with the Bahá'ís he knew.

They pored over the material with Curtis, but couldn't find what he and his mother were looking for.

Curtis was too absorbed with the Writings of Bahá'u'lláh to pursue finding an answer to his unusual experience. Instead, he plunged into the Bahá'í literature as one who had discovered precious treasure. But that wasn't enough: he attended every Bahá'í meeting he could, often returning home early in the morning, and at times perching himself under the streetlamp in front of his house, reading more of Bahá'u'lláh's Writings.

Curtis' father, who had been watching his son gravitating deeper into the Bahá'í Faith, consuming most of his waking hours with it, was determined to draw him back to what he considered was the real world. The fact that Curtis had not gone back to work irked Mr Kelsey. To him, his son had lost hold of his senses. Unable to sleep one night, he went to the bedroom window and noticed Curtis camped under the streetlight, lost in a Bahá'í book. He opened the window and cried out, 'Son! For the love of Mike, come to bed – you can read tomorrow.'

Mrs Kelsey tried to assure her husband that Curtis' ardor for Bahá'u'lláh would soon manifest itself in a more balanced way. She was right. Curtis returned to work, but his enthusiasm for the Faith never waned. In fact, he became an ardent teacher, sharing the Message whenever possible, and enjoying doing it. One day while riding with a friend on the New York subway, he decided to teach him the Faith. As the train rumbled on, and they were standing, holding onto the leather straps overhead, swaying from time to time, Curtis started talking about the Bahá'í Revelation. Though his friend seemed bored, Curtis persisted. To make a point, he reached into his coat pocket for a booklet. When he pulled it out and opened it, the words, 'The wise are they that speak not unless they find a hearing,' glared at him; Curtis quickly stuffed the booklet back into his pocket and switched topics. At the time his friend wasn't interested in the Bahá'í Faith, or any religion. The subway experience impressed upon Curtis the importance of employing wisdom in teaching and never forcing the Faith on anyone.

On April 15, 1918 Curtis received a letter from the War Department. He had been drafted into the United States Army and had only a couple of weeks to straighten out his affairs before reporting for duty in Portland, Oregon. Going into the Armed Services didn't frighten him because he sincerely felt that his country's cause in the First World War was a righteous one. The only thing that troubled him was Bahá'u'lláh's exhortation that 'it is better to be killed than to kill.' How do you convey that principle to a sergeant? he wondered. When he shared that concern with his mother, she urged him to stay close to the Teachings and seek God's guidance and protection and all would work out for the best.

While in the United States Curtis never complained about army life. Wherever he was he tried to contact the local Bahá'ís. While doing basic training at Camp Lewis, near Tacoma, Washington, he attended several meetings. It was at the first meeting that he discovered one of the effects the Faith had had on him. He described the experience in a letter to his mother: 'You know how reserved I am about talking in large groups. Well, when it comes to talking about the Revelation, I can talk for some time. In fact, I hate to stop.'

In the summer of 1918 Curtis was in France marching toward the front, still an infantryman who was used at times as a runner, carrying messages to headquarters. His application to drive trucks was turned down. Within a few days he would be in the trenches facing the Germans, and he was still a rifleman.

During a break in a long march, the company commander asked if anyone had experience in electrical wiring. Having done some work like that for his father, Curtis stepped forward and immediately became a part of a Signal Corps detachment, where he worked in repairing and setting up telephone lines on the front, often in the face of enemy gunfire. He thanked Bahá'u'lláh for saving him from having to fire his rifle.

Only six months after putting on a soldier's uniform, Curtis' feeling about the war changed. The patriotic fanfare at the Army induction center in Portland, with sweet ladies, young and old, fluttering about the recruits, handing out candies, cakes, coffee, toothbrushes and bibles, treating the young men as warrior-heroes about to launch a crusade to wipe out some mighty evil force overseas, and the bands, with their martial music, had reinforced the spirit of self-importance and self-righteousness that surged through the conscripts. They marched off to basic training, certain that the Germans were no match for them.

In France, it wasn't the endless rain and mud, the fact that Curtis' shoes and socks were always wet, having to eat cold canned beans and scrappy meat when there was anything to eat at all, and having to pick lice from his skin every day, that

FAR LEFT: Curtis' parents, Frank and Valeria Kelsey. LEFT: Curtis at the age of sixteen in Portland, Oregon. BELOW: Curtis in U.S. Army barracks, 1919. Written on the back: 'This is the kind of a castle we have on the Rhine. Curtis.'

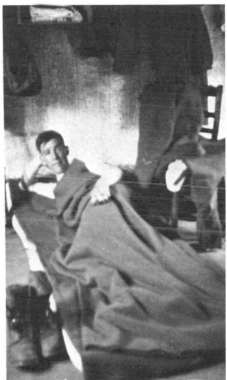

really changed his attitude. Not even having to crawl through fields searching for grass to eat for four days when the company cook was lost in battle, and eating what they found, like desperate beasts, had as much impact on him as seeing men, mostly young men, marching, always marching in long gray, spiritless lines. The more they marched, the older the troops seemed to grow, for they seemed to sense that death was hovering near; and they had no recourse to prevent that end. Hopeless men, not only the Americans, the British and French, but the Germans as well. Curtis saw lines of prisoners, bent and beaten human beings, looking very much like his buddies and himself. And they marched, too, farther and farther from their homes, without purpose, uncertain of the future. War seemed insane to Curtis. It was the Tablets of 'Abdu'l-Bahá, sent to him by his mother, which he carried throughout his army experience, that kept him from losing hope. Every day he would try to read something. On days when he couldn't read, he wrote his mother, 'The Revelation would always come to mind.'

He always felt that one day he would be home, that what he was experiencing was a phase in his life that he had to live through, and that it had some meaning, which he couldn't understand at the time. Such certitude was uncommon among the soldiers in his outfit. They were enveloped by gloom, and Curtis could understand why, for they saw no purpose in what they were doing, and all they could see and feel, day after day, was the wretchedness and human misery that results from war. For most, the only end they saw was death. This attitude prevailed even among some of the religious men.

One of Curtis' marching partners was a fuzzy-cheeked

youth from South Carolina who considered his situation hopeless. 'I know I'm going to be killed,' he told Curtis, while both men rested, after a long march, in some shell-pocked field near the Argonne front. Curtis tried to dissuade the recruit from being so negative, but the youth insisted that he was sure he would never see home again. Moments later a shell exploded nearby and a piece of shrapnel burst into the South Carolinian's forehead, knocking him into a ditch. Curtis crawled to him and saw the young man's lifeless, rigid stare.

Whenever possible Curtis tried to share the Message of Bahá'u'lláh with his fellow soldiers. Most weren't interested, and some even ridiculed him. But talking about the Faith lifted him beyond the fear that seemed to stalk the troops; it brought moments of peace. Very few soldiers listened to Curtis. But one young man was so impressed with the Message that months after the Armistice, while on vacation, he wrote to Curtis saying that after the guns had stopped firing he tried to drive the Faith out of his mind but couldn't, and that he was visiting Bahá'ís to learn more. In Paris one day while in a restaurant Curtis heard a familiar voice calling him. He turned around and saw someone he had started teaching while in basic training. The man later became a Bahá'í.

Throughout Curtis' army experience his mother wrote letters of encouragement, often mentioning the Faith, providing a Bahá'í perspective, very much like this passage from a letter dated November 15, 1918:

'Praise be to God! – your letter came to my hand the morning we heard the news that the Armistice was signed, and I wondered what you were doing, seeing and thinking, in the breaking up of the old world hurly. Only of one thing did I feel very sure, and that was that you would stand firm in the protection of 'Abdu'l-Bahá, that you would not lose faith in Him, whatever happened; and I have prayed day after day, that you might have all the experience that was for your good and which you were able to bear. Of course, we can hardly endure it to have you over there, and we want you home so bad we don't know how even to say it – but when this is all told, we are still glad that you are there, able to see at first hand what the destroyer, war, is – so that in the future, if it is God's will, you may do your part to help make war forevermore impossible. I want you to learn and grow and to see with unprejudiced eyes; and above all, I want you to do the work that will count in the days that are to follow this war, when our own America will be tested by trials which she as yet dreams little of. That is all in God's time, though not in man's, except as he through prayer and consecration, sees the truth develop in human life and knows that the false standards must first be destroyed ...'

Chapter 3

It was refreshing being home, except home now was in New Rochelle, a suburb of New York City. His father's engineering business was prospering, and the house was elegant, and there was a big new car in the garage. Curtis' younger brother Robert was attending Horace Mann, a prestigious private school for young men preparing for college. His older brother Arthur, always a dreamer, an explorer of mystical realms, who was fascinated by astrology, seemed more settled working for an advertising firm in the City. Mother's cooking was something special, even better than the fancy stuff Curtis had eaten while in Paris after the Armistice was signed. Maybe it was the home atmosphere that made Mrs Kelsey's food so delicious.

It was good being near her again, his source of comfort and assurance during his days in the Army. There was a special bond between the two, something his father couldn't fathom. Perhaps it was difficult for Frank Kelsey to understand, because his wife was more than a flesh and blood parent to Curtis: she was his spiritual parent as well.

Curtis went back to work after a couple of weeks of eating home-cooked food, driving the new car into the country for picnics with friends, seeing the Bahá'ís, who came over to shower their affection on him and to learn firsthand what the conditions were like in Europe. But even when the light of celebrity faded, life remained exciting, mainly because of his Bahá'í activity. It wasn't always meeting new people at Bahá'í gatherings that made life fun, there was a more private adventure that at times set off feelings of exaltation – and that was studying the Writings of Bahá'u'lláh and 'Abdu'l-Bahá. Through the Writings Curtis discovered new meanings to matters that once baffled him, and many educational gaps – the result of quitting school at fourteen – were filled. Gaining insight into the purpose of life, the nature of the human being, life after death and other fundamental questions was like being a prospector finding gold. The more he dug into the Writings the more insight he gained. As a result, he approached each day with enthusiasm, wondering what he would discover next, what new avenue Bahá'u'lláh would lead him to. He believed with all his heart and soul that God's help was always close. That made life exciting, but more than that, it gave him strength to solve problems, and there were to be many deeply painful ones during his seventy-six years.

It wasn't long before Curtis was elected to the Local Spiritual Assembly of New York City. Back in 1920 Bahá'ís didn't have to reside in the town where there was an Assembly in order to serve on it. Curtis was the youngest member of the Assembly, which was composed of some veteran and distinguished believers like Horace Holley, Saffa Kinney, Roy Wilhelm, Mrs Mountfort Mills and Mary

Hanford Ford. Though he respected these people, he remained independent-minded in the Assembly chamber. His strong individualistic nature was a factor. But it was more than that. He had a keen awareness of the Faith's emphasis that each Assembly member should offer his suggestion or idea free of any influence or pressure from others. And he was a stickler for following the guidelines of Bahá'í administration. He attended every meeting with his trusted book on the subject. At times some of the Assembly members teased him about his strict adherence to the book he carried. 'Here comes Kelsey with his book!' some would cry out when Curtis appeared at the Assembly meeting. Others would address him (jokingly) as 'the junior member' of the Local Spiritual Assembly.

Being only twenty-five and on an Assembly that served such a large community was frightening. Everyone seemed to know so much more than he did and everyone seemed brighter. It was the Writings that saved him. He knew that in order to be more effective on the Assembly, he would have to study the Teachings more. It was this that eventually gave him confidence, for left to his own natural inclination he would have contributed little or nothing to consultation. By nature he was a retiring person who was timid about speaking to a group of people, even a small group. The Writings set him ablaze.

Roy Wilhelm was drawn to Curtis; he admired the young man's independent spirit and the two became close friends. One reason why Curtis enjoyed going to Wilhelm's place was because it was in the country, in Teaneck, New Jersey, a town of about 4,000 people. What a difference a river can make, Curtis thought. Of course, this was before the George

Washington Bridge drew New Jersey closer to New York City. There were hills and open space in Teaneck, and a large pine grove on Roy's property, where Curtis spent quiet moments in reflection. But most of his time at Roy's was involved in producing something tangible. Both men were active people. For a while they were busy building a woodworking shop on weekends. One day while banging a nail into a board, Curtis suddenly recalled that time in Tacoma when Roy had asked him to come East to help him build a shop at his place. He sat back and laughed. Strange things do happen, he thought. But in his heart he knew that his being at Roy's wasn't strange. It was just another case of Bahá'u'lláh leading him to a new avenue. A few years back he would have considered the experience strange, even eerie.

The fact that Curtis was helping him build a woodworking shop didn't surprise Roy. Not because he had forgotten what he had said to Curtis ten years back when they were alone in the Kelsey basement. No, he had not forgotten. But Roy, despite his pragmatic nature, had learned that what is mystical can be real. He became convinced of that through an experience that shook the very roots of his conservative sensibilities.

Roy's mother was a Bahá'í, one of the earliest believers in the United States. But Roy, though tolerant of his mother's beliefs, couldn't see himself fitting into the Bahá'í pattern. He was satisfied with his life-style. He was financially secure, a respected entrepreneur. So he pursued life as he had done for years. You might say he was a creature of habit. Every work day Roy would get up at the same time, wear dark conservative suits, buy the *Herald Tribune* from the same newstand, and take the same train to Wall Street. When he returned home in the afternoon, he would take the same train, and stop off at the same flower shop to buy his mother flowers. Upon arriving home, he would regularly go to his room, remove his suit coat, replacing it with a dinner-jacket, sit on his bed to remove his shoes and put on slippers.

One day that pattern was altered, but what happened was purely involuntary. He was sitting on his bed, changing his shoes, when his room was suddenly transformed. The walls were whitewashed, and there was a divan. Standing next to Roy was a majestic figure with a long black beard, dressed in what appeared to be an oriental gown. The figure approached Roy, taking off His ring and placing it on Roy's finger and removing Roy's ring and placing it on His finger.

Roy was riveted to the bed, too startled to feel fear, so awed that he couldn't utter a word. When whatever had developed before him faded away, he tried to analyze what had happened, but he was baffled. This practical man was not prone to psychic experiences. Visions were things he heard his mother's friends talk about; and he secretly felt that half of them were less than mentally balanced.

Roy didn't tell anyone about the experience. Certainly not his friends, because they would most certainly consider him crazy; and had he related the incident to his mother, she would resume her campaign to draw him into the Bahá'í Faith. But eventually he shared his secret, despite the fact that he had planned never to reveal it. A power greater than him unlocked his heart.

When Roy's mother received word that she could go to the Holy Land to see 'Abdu'l-Bahá, she asked if her son would escort her. It didn't take much to persuade him to go along, because he didn't want his mother travelling alone to a strange and dangerous place halfway around the world. Seeing the Master in 1907 was difficult, because he was still a prisoner of the Ottoman Empire.

So when they reached the Haifa area, they had to be smuggled into the Master's house at night, lest the enemies of the Faith and the Covenant-breakers spotted the Wilhelms. When 'Abdu'l-Bahá saw Roy, He approached him with outstretched arms and hugged him so hard that Roy thought several of his ribs had been cracked. The very proper and Victorian Roy had never been hugged by a man before. It happened so swiftly that he didn't have time to retreat from the Master's embrace. Besides, the hug convinced him that he was most welcome, and whatever reservations he had about the safety and sanity of the place vanished.

Upon the urging of the Master, Roy went to 'Akká and Bahjí. Before reaching Bahjí, the carriage he was riding in stopped at the Garden of Riḍván. There, one of the Persians led him to a small white house where Bahá'u'lláh had stayed whenever He visited the Garden. As he entered, he sensed that he had been there before. It was the same room in which that extraordinary figure exchanged rings with him. Roy jumped back, retreating quickly to the garden, shaken. He could no longer hide the secret; he felt a strong urge to share this experience with 'Abdu'l-Bahá – nobody else.

'You had a spiritual experience,' the Master told Roy. 'Bahá'u'lláh had wedded you to His Faith.'

From that day on Mr Roy C. Wilhelm was a Bahá'í, never entertaining even the thought of divorcing himself from the Faith.

Curtis learned from Roy, mostly by example. Steadfastness and firmness in the Covenant seemed to be reflected in almost everything Roy did. The Faith was the primary force in his life. He knew what Bahá'u'lláh represented to the world; without Him there was death. And he understood 'Abdu'l-Bahá's relationship to the Blessed Beauty. What the Master said was what Bahá'u'lláh would say. When 'Abdu'l-Bahá asked Roy to do something, he did it without hesitation. And the Master knew how strong Roy's faith was. That's why he was often called upon to do what most other believers weren't mature enough to do.

During one of the Master's visits to New York City in 1912, he called Roy at his office, asking him to come to the Hotel Ansonia where He was staying. Roy left immediately. When he entered the presence of 'Abdu'l-Bahá, he noticed a number of friends, including several Persians, seated around the room. The Master had Roy sit in the middle of the room, and began to talk to him about the importance of obedience, in a reprimanding manner, waving his finger at Roy. Most other people would have whimpered and cowered, or stomped out of the room; but Roy didn't flinch. He was puzzled, but never questioned the Master.

Actually, 'Abdu'l-Bahá had Roy submit to the tongue-lashing in order to reach a Persian believer who was in the room and needed spiritual shoring-up, because he was drifting toward Covenant-breaking. The true target of 'Abdu'l-Bahá's Message was reached and he remained firm in the Faith. In time, Roy learned what purpose he had served that day at the Hotel Ansonia.

Roy's devotion was reflected in the time and energy and money he spent for the Cause. Curtis never forgot the image of Roy Wilhelm, millionaire, leading coffee entrepreneur, in his office after midnight, hunched over a typewriter, dressed in an overcoat, because the heat had been turned off in the office building, making copies of the latest Tablets from the Master. He made hundreds of copies and had them circulated throughout the country.

Before the establishment of a publishing trust, Roy had a variety of pamphlets printed, which he would give to the believers and hand out wherever he went. It was one of these pamphlets that helped a young Pittsburgh newspaperwoman, Miss Martha Root, to become a Bahá'í. Roy handed it to her in a Philadelphia cafeteria while eating lunch.

There was a time, however, Curtis recalls, when Roy's obedience bordered on the edge of comedy. 'Abdu'l-Bahá was familiar with some of the American idioms and would use them at times in writing to some of the American believers. On one occasion the Master urged him to work at becoming a 'straight shooter.'

Roy's immediate reaction was to purchase a couple of pistols and set up two targets in the backyard of his Teaneck home. After several shooting sessions, some of the neighbors expressed concern. When Curtis discovered what was going on, he pointed out that perhaps the Master meant something else by Roy becoming a 'straight shooter.' 'Maybe,' Curtis suggested, 'you should be more direct in your business practices.' Roy adopted Curtis' interpretation and adjusted his business practices, practices that were considered quite normal on Wall Street.

Being a Bahá'í in New York City after World War One was exciting in many ways, and not only because many messages from 'Abdu'l-Bahá arrived there first. The city itself was alive, full of promise of better days ahead. The war was over, and the feeling that there would be no more wars was a realistic and logical assumption. For how could any sane human being condone the repetition of what had convulsed Europe and the Middle East from 1914 to 1918? Humanity, most people believed, had learned its lesson. In 1920 people were channeling considerable energy into searching for ways to generate eternal happiness, to create lasting peace. All sorts of fads, philosophies and ideologies flourished in cosmopolitan New York.

In a way, the Faith benefited from this spirit of inquiry that seemed to be sweeping through the city. It wasn't uncommon for 200 or more people to show up at a regular Sunday public meeting. In the crowd there was usually a rich assortment of types: Bolsheviks, socialists of varying schools of thought, air-eaters, vegetarians, suffragettes, swamis, anarchists, poor and rich, black and white, atheists and 'holy rollers,' even adherents of a cult that ate only nuts – and only in trees. (The Green Acre Bahá'í school in Maine was a favorite gathering place in the summer for these nut-eaters, because of the many trees there.) And there were raw food enthusiasts, financiers, theosophists, metaphysical doctors and literary notables like Sinclair Lewis and Dorothy Thompson, who were open admirers of the Faith. Conventional Presbyterians, Catholics and Jews showed up as well.

Of course, not all of the people who attended meetings joined the Faith. But there was something appealing about it. Not many of those who showed up were aware of why they were attracted to the meetings. They sensed the oneness, the unity, the love. When they attended a Bahá'í meeting, most seekers felt accepted regardless of what they looked like or professed philosophically. And there were those who had to know the cause of the unusual social dynamic they were witnessing and feeling. So they probed – and discovered Bahá'u'lláh.

But there were others, like Hooper Harris – who served on the New York Assembly with Curtis – who, like Roy Wilhelm, were drawn to Bahá'u'lláh in a most unconventional manner. Curtis often felt how fortunate the friends were to have such a powerful advocate of the Faith in their midst. In some respects Hooper Harris was a factor in Curtis' devotion to studying the Teachings, for he wanted to be equipped to refute the attackers of the Faith, to share with eloquence the healing and unifying Message of Bahá'u'lláh with those who didn't know about the Cause. Something as magnificent as the Faith deserved to be expressed superlatively. And Hooper Harris was a perfect model for young Curtis to follow.

Though born in New York City, he was brought up in Nashville, Tennessee, and became a lawyer in Alabama. After marrying Sarah Gertrude Rawls in Birmingham, they moved to New York where he became one of the city's outstanding court reporters. Though the possessor of a brilliant mind, as a young man he had a natural suspicion of anything that gave the slightest appearance of unorthodoxy. When his wife became a Bahá'í, he was outraged. So vehement was his dislike of the Bahá'í Faith that he vowed to disprove it. One Sunday morning he told his wife he was going to his office on Wall Street to write a treatise disproving the claim of Bahá'u'lláh. When he reached his office, he took off his jacket and sat down at his desk. But he couldn't write a thing. His hand wouldn't move. It wasn't paralysis. He tried again. Still no motion. He placed the pencil on the pad and stretched out on the couch, wondering what was happening to him. It was something that he had never experienced before. 'God,' he said to himself, 'help me.' No sooner had he said that than a figure appeared, seeming to emerge from the wall – a beautiful figure, smiling. As Hooper peered at whatever stood before him, he felt his animosity toward the Faith being drawn from his being and he was helpless to stop what was happening to him. He left the pad and pencil on the desk, put on his jacket and proceeded to walk home, about five miles, to 103rd street where he lived, never thinking about the distance, only about how good he felt when he thought about Bahá'u'lláh.

Mr Harris became an ardent believer. Working for the Cause took preference over everything else in his life. He loved to teach; and he was so good at it. No place seemed to restrict Hooper Harris when it came to sharing the Message of Bahá'u'lláh. Curtis often wondered how Hooper, who was so dignified, was able to withstand the heckling when he spoke from a soap-box in New York's Columbus Circle. The Bolsheviks seemed to be the most abusive, often cursing him, jeering him, for they had no tolerance for anyone connected with religion, and the mention of God generated hisses and boos. But the people who gathered at that street-corner eventually grew to respect him. In fact, the Bolsheviks invited him to speak at their meeting-place in Greenwich Village, which was a large, dimly lit, unheated loft, reeking of garlic and unwashed bodies. Curtis had a vivid recollection of the place, because the thought of not getting out of there alive flashed through his mind time and time again, as he stood near the dauntless Hooper Harris, facing about 200 hostile faces. The chairman, who was wielding a carpenter's hammer for a gavel, had difficulty quieting the crowd.

Everyone seemed to have something to say, and no one seemed willing to listen. The louder one spoke the more respect one received. After about twenty clouts of the hammer on a terribly dented table, the noise level lowered and Hooper was introduced to a chorus of boos. But that didn't worry Hooper. Curtis was impressed with the way Hooper handled the crowd. Seemingly oblivious of their contempt, he spoke to them as if they were sympathetic to his cause. He.didn't shrink from talking about God; but he did it in a way that didn't alienate the audience. His knowledge of Marxism helped, for he wove Marxist terms into his talk; and his approach was empathetic. In other words, he acknowledged why the audience was attracted to the philosophy of Karl Marx and expressed respect for their decision to embrace Marxism. He truly understood why they took such a step. But he was unyielding in upholding the validity of the existence of God. His sincerity, empathy, mental brilliance and faith helped to penetrate some hearts in the crowd. After Hooper's talk, Curtis remembered, a rabbi, who had left his synagogue to join the Communist party, approached Hooper, thanking him for restoring his faith in God. The man went back to his synagogue to serve his people, and for many years stayed in touch with Hooper.

Perhaps the most courageous believer Curtis knew was a frail-looking woman, Mary Hanford Ford. To many she resembled a dainty Dresden doll. But appearances can be deceiving. For Curtis remembered this old lady leaving her New York City home in a snowstorm to speak at a fireside in West Englewood, New Jersey, and never complaining; showing up at the meeting, beaming joy, happy that she had the opportunity to share with people a Message from God.

And people listened to her, because they knew she practiced what she was talking about.

From Louis Gregory, Curtis learned what humility and wisdom were. Aware of Mr Gregory's reputation as a teacher, Curtis stood in awe of this Washington D.C. attorney, whom the Master said was 'like pure Gold.'

He was flabbergasted when Mr Gregory approached him one day in Green Acre and asked if Curtis and he might work together in teaching a course at the summer school. 'Me and Louis Gregory,' Curtis thought to himself, 'sharing teaching duties? Incredible!'

They did the course together, and Curtis was never made to feel inadequate. In fact, through his association with Mr Gregory he gained more confidence as a teacher. Louis had a way of getting you to do more than you thought you could do; and it was done through consultation, not by his telling you what was right and wrong.

Watching Urban LeDoux practice his Faith was an unforgettable lesson in serving one's fellow human being. Mr LeDoux, a French Canadian and former Canadian diplomat, called himself Mr Zero. For he viewed himself as nothing and everyone else as greater than himself. Even the New York newspapers that covered his antics referred to him as Mr Zero. There were times when he would literally give someone the shirt off his back. His desire to serve others, especially the down-trodden, stemmed from the time he embraced Bahá'u'lláh. After resigning his diplomatic post, Mr LeDoux opened a soup-kitchen and boarding-house for those living in the streets of New York's skid row. He collected clothing for these people, tried to counsel them, light the lamp of spirit in their hearts. Curtis remembered

how hard Mr LeDoux worked, rarely taking a day off.
Urban's greatest pleasure was seeing the people he tried to
help discover hope, a reason for living. And many did, some
becoming Bahá'ís.

Mr LeDoux was a big, strong man, very much an activist. If
he noticed an injustice, he didn't hesitate to alter the
situation.

Upset with political corruption, he went to Washington
D.C. and became one of the first White House pickets. He
walked back and forth in front of the presidential mansion
carrying a lantern and a placard which read, 'Looking for an
honest man.'

All of these outstanding figures – Louis Gregory, Roy
Wilhelm, Mary Hanford Ford, Urban LeDoux, Hooper
Harris and others like Saffa and Vaffa Kinney, and Horace
Holley – helped Curtis to see more of the reality of the Faith.
Although different, these people had one thing in common:
they put their Faith first in their lives. And Curtis believed
that this was why they were successful in what they wanted to
do most – and that was to serve the Cause of God. They were
audacious, courageous, doing things that they naturally
would have shied away from doing had they not made a total
commitment to living by the Covenant of Bahá'u'lláh.

Chapter 4

Whenever Curtis wasn't in the field, he would try to have lunch with Roy in lower Manhattan. At one of these meetings, Roy invited Curtis to come to his office, because he had something important to ask him. Why not ask me at the restaurant? Curtis wondered. But then there was always an air of mystery about Roy. It was a quirk that didn't deter Curtis; in fact he found it exciting, because Roy was the kind of person who made things happen.

When the two were alone, Roy nonchalantly said, 'How would you like to go to Haifa to do some work for the Master?'

At first Curtis thought it was a joke, but Roy appeared serious. 'Well, of course,' Curtis replied. 'But Haifa is far away, and I don't have the money to make the trip and back.'

It was a response Roy had hoped for and said, 'You never know about these things – strange things happen.'

Curtis wanted to laugh, because he had heard Roy make the same statement in Tacoma. And what had happened to him that evening in his workshop had radically transformed his life. While walking back to his office, Curtis was flush with anticipation, wondering what was going to unfold next.

Several weeks later Curtis received a cablegram from Haifa. He handled it with care, making sure not to damage the contents inside the envelope. When he finally opened it, he read: CURTIS KELSEY PERMITTED, signed 'Abdu'l-Bahá 'Abbás. As he studied the cablegram, a strong urge swept over him to start preparing for the trip right away. He felt he had to reach Haifa as soon as possible. But there were so many things to put in order. He knew his father, who was also his professional boss, would oppose his leaving for the Near East, especially for an indefinite period of time. Traveling thousands of miles would be costly; where would he get the money to do that? But for some reason, he felt he would get to Haifa. One of the first things he did was prepare his newly acquired Model T Ford – something he was deeply attached to – so that he could sell it. He drove to downtown New Rochelle where a group of young men usually congregated, and showed off the freshly polished automobile. When no one showed any interest, he started driving away. But someone in the crowd called for Curtis to stop, stating that he was interested in checking the car out. He said he would buy it for $150 if it could climb a certain hill in town. Fortunately, Curtis had cleaned the spark plugs that day and the car was able to go up the hill in high gear. Though Curtis sold a few other possessions, he still didn't have enough money to make the trip. There were no buyers for some of the other things he had for sale, things he valued highly. But at that point in Curtis' life there was nothing more precious than to be with 'Abdu'l-Bahá.

After approaching most possible sources of money, and

failing to secure any more funds, Bahá'u'lláh led Curtis back
to Roy. At lunch one afternoon, Roy had asked Curtis how
he was progressing in obtaining money for his trip to the Holy
Land. Though admitting that he was short in collecting the
amount needed, Curtis expressed optimism that he'd soon
get what he needed. All he wanted, he said, was enough to
get there, and he would worry about how he would get back
later.

Roy knew Curtis would never ask the Master for the fare,
though He would gladly have paid for his way. He sensed that
Curtis was in a dilemma; and he was aware of Curtis' strong
streak of independence. So in a tactful way, he persuaded
Curtis to take $500 from him, explaining that it was only so
that his trip could be financed. Because Curtis respected
Roy's judgement, he took the money.

But there was another obstacle to going: Curtis' father.
Frank Kelsey felt a trip to the Orient would retard Curtis'
professional development. He also didn't want to lose his
son's services, because Curtis was a responsible supervisor in
the field. In a meeting he had with Curtis, he employed every
rational approach he could think of to dissuade his son from
going to Haifa. When that didn't crack Curtis' resolve, Frank
Kelsey told him how he really felt: 'Son, you must be taking
leave of your senses. Here you are, just getting started in
your work and now you plan to make this long trip and do
that work for that little old man in Haifa; and they are not
going to pay you for it.'

Though Curtis was hurt by his father's reference to
'Abdu'l-Bahá as 'a little old man,' he knew his father didn't
understand who the Master was, and at that point no amount
of explanation could open his eyes and heart. 'Father,' he

said, 'I must make this trip, but I haven't the time to explain why – now.'

'If you must go,' Mr Kelsey said, 'don't expect any financial help from me.'

After considerable checking, Curtis discovered there were no steamers going directly to Haifa. He had to settle for a voyage to France, where he would try to arrange connections to the Holy Land. He wanted to get there as fast as possible, so that he could be with the Master. The prospect of being near 'Abdu'l-Bahá, listening to Him speak, watching Him doing things, eating with Him, working with Him, was almost too much to bear. If only he could wave some magical wand that would transport him to Haifa in an instant. But in 1921 airplanes weren't crossing oceans. The ship was still the fastest way. Without complications, it took three weeks to reach Haifa; and all he was assured of was reaching France. Every travel agent he contacted said he would never make it in three weeks, that he would be lucky if he made it in a month.

But getting to the Holy Land in time wasn't the only thing Curtis had to worry about. Several days before he was to leave, Roy revealed the primary purpose for the trip ... and that set off feelings of anxiety, even doubt about his ability to carry out the assignment. He was to design and install electrical systems at the Shrines of the Báb and Bahá'u'lláh and in 'Abdu'l-Bahá's house. Since there was no electricity in Bahjí and Haifa, he would have to install lighting generators at the three sites. It was something that required more experience than he had, Curtis thought. Maybe an electrical engineer should be doing the job, not an elementary school dropout.

When Curtis shared his reservations with Roy, Roy didn't seem disturbed. In fact he expressed confidence that his young friend would do what had to be done. Just like Roy, Curtis thought. The man operates on a different level, and when he says that strange things happen, he knows they do. Soon Curtis realized that the level Roy was operating on was faith, and he couldn't deny that power.

When Roy explained why the Master wanted the project done, Curtis knew he couldn't back out. Besides, Roy had organized things so that Curtis had no alternative but to go. His steamship ticket had been purchased, and 'Abdu'l-Bahá was awaiting his arrival.

What set off the project was Roy's reading of these words of the Báb in which He bemoans the fact that while incarcerated in the fortress of Mákú He didn't have even a lamp in His cell:

'How veiled are ye, O My creatures ... who, without any right have consigned Him [the Báb] unto a mountain [Mákú], not one of whose inhabitants is worthy of mention ... With Him, which is with Me, there is no one except him who is one of the Letters of the Living of My Book. In His presence, which is My presence, there is not at night even a lighted lamp! And yet, in places [of worship] which in varying degrees reach out unto Him, unnumbered lamps are shining! All that is on earth hath been created for Him, and all partake with delight of His benefits, and yet they are so veiled from Him as to refuse Him even a lamp!'

Roy was so moved by the statement, he immediately wrote the Master, asking for permission to send a lighting plant to Haifa to light the Shrine of the Báb. Shortly after sending the letter, he received a cablegram from 'Abdu'l-Bahá, stating that three plants were necessary. Roy responded instantly. In a matter of weeks, the machinery was on its way to Mount Carmel.

The lighting plants remained in Haifa for about a year, untouched. Some of the friends in the United States were aware of the project and tried to help expedite it. One Californian believer sent a young electrical engineer over to do the work, but the Master sent him back, stating that it wasn't time yet. A Persian, Ḥusayn-i-Kahrubáyí (meaning Ḥusayn the electrician) also traveled to Haifa to ask 'Abdu'l-Bahá if he could work on the project. The Master said that when the time was right, he would be called to assist – and he was.

The dock workers serving on the steamship *Olympic* probably thought Curtis Kelsey was a celebrity. A crowd of Bahá'ís came out to bid 'Abdu'l-Bahá's electrician farewell. Many of the people knew Curtis, but there were others who didn't. All were there hoping at least to catch a glimpse of someone who was going to be so close to their Lord. How they longed to be in Curtis' position. They handed him notes and gifts for 'Abdu'l-Bahá. Some asked him to pray for them or someone special at the Holy Tombs.

Curtis' parents were in the crowd that surged toward him. But Mrs Kelsey didn't have the strength to push through the crowd. She stayed back, unable even to see her son's face, while her husband pressed toward Curtis; he had to give him something important. When he reached his son, he handed him an envelope and simply said 'Good-bye,' and slipped back into the crowd. In glancing at the envelope, Curtis noticed a note attached to it, which asked that he not open the envelope until he was aboard the steamer.

Mrs Kelsey had already said her farewell that morning when she gave Curtis a gift, a Graflex camera with lots of film. She had asked him to take many pictures of the Holy Land, particularly the places where 'Abdu'l-Bahá visited, the paths He walked. There was nothing she wanted more than to be with the Master; but she felt her husband would resist any attempt to go to Haifa. She didn't want to cause any discord in the household, so she let the matter rest. She would have to make her pilgrimage through her son.

Curtis remained on the deck, waving to the friends on the wharf, as long as he could see them. He was back on the Atlantic Ocean, that vast body of water he had crossed twice in recent years. But now he was heading for France, not to fight a war, but to find the next step in his journey to serve the most powerful force for peace on Earth.

When Curtis opened the envelope his father had handed him, he found $250. The gift didn't surprise him, because he knew his father cared for him. But the money symbolized a change of heart on the part of his father – that he finally respected Curtis' commitment to serving 'Abdu'l-Bahá, even though he couldn't subscribe to the Bahá'í Teachings. Now he could proceed without feeling guilty that he had disappointed his father terribly, or abandoned him.

Of all his sons, Frank Kelsey respected Curtis the most. He wished that he could be as close with him as Curtis was with Valeria. During the war years, Frank Kelsey worried, even brooded over his son's welfare, especially in battle. Often when Mrs Kelsey cleaned her husband's study she would discover the name Curtis written a number of times along the margins of his business papers.

Roy Wilhelm had wired the Master that Curtis Kelsey

would reach the Holy Land in three weeks, and Curtis knew that. The first few days he was heartened by the progress the ship was making. There was lots of sunshine, and whatever wind blew was coming from the west, thus helping to quicken the ship's pace. It was an enjoyable trip. Sleeping in a private state room was a lot different from trying to sleep in a hammock in a cavernous room below deck, next to groaning engines, with about 500 other soldiers. The food, unlike that dispensed on the military ship, was delicious.

As the *Olympic* approached the English coast, visibility diminished. The ship had steamed into thick fog. Though virtually stalled, Curtis was only about 100 miles from Cherbourg, France, his landing point. He was certain the fog would soon lift. But when a day passed and the fog persisted, Curtis' fear of not reaching Haifa in time surfaced. About twenty hours later, when visibility improved, the *Olympic* resumed its regular speed.

Afraid that he was behind his time-schedule, Curtis practically ran to the steamship ticket-office when he left the *Olympic*. But there he ran into another barrier: the agent said it would be weeks before he could book passage to Alexandria, Egypt, where he had to take a train to Haifa. The agent encouraged Curtis to relax, go to Paris, have a good time – to do anything else would be a waste of energy.

Curtis heeded his intuition rather than the agent's advice and headed for Naples by train. It was night-time when the train entered Italy. Curtis was asleep in his berth when a pounding on his door awoke him. He scrambled out of bed and opened the door, and there standing in front of him were three policemen, who ordered him to open his trunk. Puzzled and anxious, Curtis tried to find out why they were searching his things, making him feel like a criminal. He was incensed. But the policemen ignored his attempts to find out what was happening. They rifled through his belongings, and when they discovered a small motor he was carrying to Haifa for the lighting project, they grew more animated. The policemen checked it over carefully, talking in Italian.

Perhaps, Curtis thought, he should have declared the motor at Customs. Maybe because he didn't do that, he would be deported, or worse yet, be locked up in jail.

The policemen placed the motor back in the trunk, excused themselves in English and slipped quietly out of Curtis' sleeping-cabin.

Curtis' encounter with the steamship office in Naples was as frustrating as his experience in France. When he told the agent that he would return the following day to check out shipping possibilities, he was told not to bother for there was no possibility of getting aboard a ship headed for the Near East. 'I know my business,' the agent protested. 'Nothing will happen, believe me. Now why don't you tell me where you are staying and I'll call you should something materialize.'

Two days later Curtis received a call at his hotel. It was the agent: 'Mr Kelsey, how did you know the *Esperia* would stop here?'

'I had no idea it would,' Curtis said.

'Well, it diverted its course in order to drop off a first-class passenger who had developed appendicitis. Would you like to take his place?'

'Of course, I'll be right down.'

Cruising on the Mediterranean was an improvement on the Atlantic. The ship seemed to glide through the deep, dark blue water, rarely encountering a wave. It was like sailing on one of those Maine lakes that Curtis used to visit on long summer weekend outings. Overhead the summer sun blazed, never obscured by clouds. For Curtis, every day at sea was golden; it reminded him of playing on those Long Island beaches that he and his family used to frequent. Of course, not having to worry about making a shipping connection to the Holy Land helped to make the voyage on the *Esperia* more relaxed. But the fact that this problem had been solved, plus the idyllic weather, didn't lull Curtis into forgetting the purpose of his trip. In fact, from time to time, between shuffle-board games and conversation with fellow passengers, his stomach would stiffen whenever he thought of the responsibility he had to carry out in the Holy Land. Who was going to help him? he wondered; and he was concerned about the source of supplies. As far as he knew, Palestine was a primitive place, a sort of pre-industrial-age land. True, Roy Wilhelm had shipped materials, but something was bound to happen which no one had planned for. Having worked on scores of construction projects, Curtis had learned that there is no such thing as a perfect plan. This challenge was different from any other, for it wasn't for some corporation, or even his father, who was a formidable perfectionist. To Curtis, it was like working for God. Everything he was to do had to be outstanding, flawless.

Meeting Mr Charles Dana helped Curtis to divert his attention from his forthcoming task. Mr Dana, a tall, slender, gray-haired gentleman, and a Presbyterian, directed a missionary service in the Middle East. Since he was based in Beirut, he would be travelling all the way to Haifa with Curtis. Beirut was on the same railroad line, about ninety miles north of Haifa.

When Mr Dana discovered why Curtis was going to Palestine, he revealed that he knew several Bahá'ís associated with the University of Beirut, and that he was impressed with their scholarship and character. 'What puzzles me,' he told Curtis, 'is how the Bahá'í students are able to persuade Muslims to accept the teachings of Jesus Christ when the missionaries have virtually failed to make any inroads among the followers of Muḥammad.'

'Well,' Curtis said, 'Bahá'ís are successful with attracting Muslims to their Faith, because they don't belittle the Teachings of Muḥammad. In fact, they hold them sacred.'

'But what about their acceptance of Jesus Christ?'

'That's no problem for a Muslim, because he already accepts Jesus. Muḥammad, Himself, stated to His followers that they must embrace all of the Jewish prophets, including Jesus.'

Curtis was surprised that Mr Dana was unaware of the fact that Muslims accepted Jesus, for he had spent many years in the Middle East. It was something he should have known, Curtis felt. Because if you are going to try to persuade people to adopt your religion, you must know something about their religion, not the rituals and trappings, but the central teachings. Perhaps, Curtis thought, Mr Dana and his associates felt it wasn't important to know about what they thought was false doctrine. Despite Mr Dana's feelings about Islám, Curtis found him charming, a real gentleman, who sincerely felt that he was doing God's work.

Mr Dana must have been impressed with Curtis, because he stayed close to the young American, who knew so much about religion and wasn't a clergyman. Most Americans he knew who weren't ordained ministers or priests never knew much about religion, especially religions other than their own.

In a way, being close to Mr Dana proved helpful to Curtis, because he learned much about the cultures of the Palestine area, practical things like how to barter with merchants and what the native food was like.

The two men traveled together all the way to Haifa. When they reached Alexandria, they didn't have to wait long for the simple Turkish narrow-gauge railroad train, which Mr Dana had taken numerous times. It was only a few hours' wait, time to absorb the sounds and smells of the Near East. But Alexandria wasn't typically Arab. It was a city with modern hotels. Palm trees, all right, but carefully planted in neat rows along the waterfront. But the language was different, and many men wore the fez and many women wore the veil; and there were a few camels in the downtown traffic.

Reaching the railroad station was easy; all Curtis had to do was stay close to Mr Dana.

Curtis didn't mind the bumpy ride, because there was so much to see. When they reached Cairo, Curtis found himself in a teeming metropolis, with its hundreds of minarets stretching into the sky, and hawks and vultures continually circled certain sections of the ancient city. East of Cairo, Curtis sensed ancient history – Moses leading the followers of Jehovah, the Hebrews, Egyptian slaves for nearly 400 years, toward the Promised Land. When he reached the Suez Canal and the train rattled across the bridge to Sinai, he thought of Moses and his brethren daring to cross the Red Sea with Pharaoh's soldiers in pursuit.

Sections of the Sinai reminded Curtis of southern Utah: craggy, treeless mountains and lots of rock on the sandy flat areas. From time to time they would pass a column of Bedouin nomads mounted on camels, and crumbling Coptic Christian monasteries that seemed to have been sculpted out of the hot native sands. The Old Testament seemed to come alive, for it was through the region the train was crossing that Moses had led the Hebrews toward the Holy Land.

Haifa in September 1921 was nothing like 'Abdu'l-Bahá said it would be like in the future, a metropolis, extending around the Bay of 'Akká. When Curtis and Mr Dana stepped off the train, they found themselves in a village which probably looked like a village from the days of Jesus. There were Arab women carrying jars of water on their heads, merchants selling their wares in the open, Arab men gathered in the shade, smoking bubble pipes, a couple of camels tied to a post and unbothered by the scorching sun. Mount Carmel was a huge limestone rock, covered with scrubby vegetation, with a few houses at its base; the Shrine of the Báb was a light-colored stone structure, with a flat roof, as bare as a fortress. Near the top of the mountain was the Carmelite Monastery, which had been established centuries ago by the Roman Catholic Church to watch for Christ's return; He was supposed to return on a cloud. Being in Haifa was like stepping back in time. Certainly a different world from the Woolworth Building and its sleek elevators.

Mr Dana didn't get back on the train. He would take the later one for Beirut. Curious about the Bahá'í Faith, he walked up Mount Carmel to visit the Shrine of the Báb. Curtis never saw him again.

Waiting at the train station were Fujita and Dr Luṭfu'lláh Ḥakím, two young men serving the Master, one Japanese, the other of Persian-Jewish background, in a high buckboard wagon that 'Abdu'l-Bahá would ride in, when He wasn't walking or riding a donkey. Evidently they knew who Curtis was, because he was the only young American to emerge from the train, and he was the only one who stopped to gaze at Mount Carmel. When Curtis heard his name called, he turned to see two short men approaching. Obviously Bahá'ís, he thought. Who else would know his name? Perhaps Roy had sent his picture to the Master, and they were able to identify him by it.

Both men were smiling and waving. While Curtis waved back, he wondered if he would be able to communicate with them, for he knew only English. He remembered how difficult it was to use the several French and German survival sentences he had learned in order to negotiate his way through post-war France and Germany as an American soldier. He especially had trouble pronouncing foreign sounding words. And those were from European languages. Imagine how he would mutilate an oriental language. But Curtis' anxiety soon passed. Both men spoke English, with thick Japanese and Persian accents.

For Curtis it was an unusual greeting. Though outwardly these men appeared so different from the people he knew back home, they seemed like members of his family. It was instantaneous comradeship. He had seen a few Persians before in America, but had never met a Japanese. Despite his basic shyness, there was no sense of uneasiness, no pangs of self-consciousness. Sitting in the wagon with Fujita and Luṭfu'lláh Ḥakím, heading for the Master's house, was as natural as riding in his family's car with his parents and brothers. The three men, who shared the same room while in the Holy Land, were to grow very close.

The buckboard wagon came to a halt in front of a large stone house that faced the Bay of Haifa. It was the Pilgrim House, Curtis was told, where the pilgrims stayed while they visited 'Abdu'l-Bahá. Curtis, holding two suitcases, stood in the road for a moment looking at the building, wondering what it was going to be like standing face to face with the Master. He had read many of His Tablets and heard pilgrims talk about their meetings with Him; and there were those times when he had daydreamed of being in the Master's presence. Even when he received the cablegram from Haifa, the thought that he, Curtis Kelsey, would be with 'Abdu'l-Bahá didn't seem real.

Dr Ḥakím urged Curtis to enter the house, because the Master was waiting for him. As they entered, they were greeted by two ladies, one from the East, the other from the West, and were ushered to a large table in the front room. On it was the luncheon, a large platter of Persian pilau, with curried lamb, chopped nuts and candied orange peel; saffron was sprinkled on it. Small glasses of tea and bowls of yogurt were next to each plate. Unleavened bread was piled on a dish.

Everyone was standing and chatting, mainly about Curtis' trip from New York City, when suddenly a door opened, and 'Abdu'l-Bahá appeared, heading for Curtis; He was dressed in a cream-colored 'abá and white turban, and His eyes were smiling. The Master shook Curtis' hand and said, 'Marḥabá! Marḥabá!' (You are welcome! You are welcome!) After washing his hands in a bowl of water that Fujita had brought over, He had everyone sit around the table. 'Abdu'l-Bahá had Curtis sit next to Him and asked how the friends were faring in New York, and how he liked Haifa. When Curtis replied that he liked the atmosphere there, the Master said, looking beyond everyone at the table, 'You feel this way because the prophets of the past have visited and walked in this area.' Then he turned to Curtis and asked, 'Did you notice how easy it was to get here?'

Curtis hesitated for a moment. 'Yes,' he said, 'I had noticed this.' Immediately after making that statement, Curtis realized that he had reached Haifa in twenty days, the time he had allotted himself to get to Haifa. Amazing, he thought, considering what all the experts had told him. As he ate the pilau, Curtis knew that he had been given special assistance in reaching the Holy Land.

After lunch, the Master suggested that Curtis rest for a few hours. This was the local custom, and as Curtis soon learned, it was a wise practice, because from noon to three was the hottest time of the day, making work difficult. In fact, all of the businesses closed in the afternoon, opening at dusk.

Shortly after entering the small room he shared with Fujita and Dr Ḥakím, which was next to the rear door of the Pilgrim house, a young woman came by with a branch bearing about ten oranges. It was something the Master had asked her to give Curtis.

None of the Bahá'ís in Haifa lived in luxury. The rooms where people slept were small, and the beds, which were made of iron, had boards on them and flat three-quarter-inch-thick mattresses that did little to cushion the hardness. Netting was wrapped around the beds to keep the mosquitos from poking at your flesh. Simple white curtains were on the windows. In the room where Curtis stayed, which was only fourteen-foot-square, there were three dressers, one for each occupant. Fujita's large trunk seemed to dominate the room; it was filled with clothes, which he enjoyed wearing when he was going to parties in California and Michigan. He even had a fancy white-tie tuxedo with tails. From time to time, Fujita would have Luṭfu'lláh Ḥakím and Curtis sit down, and he would go to his trunk, open it and exclaim, 'Look, all dressed up and no place to go!' That never failed to make Curtis laugh.

It took a few days before Curtis became accustomed to resting during the afternoon, a period of time that was considered peak working hours back home. Of course, his roommates had no trouble dozing off. Fujita had been in Haifa for two years and Dr Ḥakím was from that part of the world. During his first siesta, Curtis tried to sleep; he stretched out on the bed, but his first meeting with 'Abdu'l-Bahá had stirred him. Being with the Master was more than he had imagined. 'Abdu'l-Bahá's nobility was obvious, but he didn't flaunt it. In His presence, Curtis didn't feel like cowering; instead he felt at ease, completely accepted and totally loved. Before meeting 'Abdu'l-Bahá there were times when Curtis felt unworthy of being with Him. But he never experienced that feeling when he was with the Master. In fact, he was forgetful of self. Later on in life, in reflecting on why he always felt at ease with 'Abdu'l-Bahá, Curtis realized that the Master wouldn't allow you to feel unworthy, whatever your station in life, be you pauper or potentate. Being with the Master you discovered you had value; you knew you weren't being judged; you experienced freedom – something you thought you had experienced back home, but really hadn't.

Every week Curtis would receive at least one letter from his mother, sometimes two. Judging by the dates of her letters, she had started writing the day her son left for Haifa. Like the letters she wrote during the war, they were newsy, often witty, full of genuine encouragement and advice given as a gift. It was uncanny, Curtis felt, that her letters often addressed a concern that he was keeping to himself. For example, even after the first few days in Haifa, Curtis remained anxious about his assignment. But after pondering this section of one of his mother's letters, dated September 7, 1921, his anxiety diminished: 'I know you will have so much to do and see, and that your spirit will be constantly fed, so that you will receive good from every direction, even in your physical labors and complex situations, for you will turn always to 'Abdu'l-Bahá, and you will let 'Abdu'l-Bahá be the real builder of the lighting system ...'

Whatever the Master asked Curtis to do, he did it immediately, without reservation or hesitation. But he wasn't asked to do much during the first two weeks he was in the Holy Land. In fact, he had the freedom to do whatever he wished. So he went about fixing whatever needed repair at the World Center. When he checked out the garage, he found two automobiles – a big Cunningham and a Ford. They had been sent to Haifa by some American friends. Neither of the cars was functioning. In a few days, Curtis had the vehicles operating and he took the Master for several rides around the Mount Carmel area.

There was no automobile traffic in Haifa in 1921 – only one other person, a young Arab, had a car. The ancient stone roads were really twisting alleyways. Curtis, who had a passion for cars and speed, found negotiating the roads an exciting challenge, except when he drove the Master about. Then he was extra careful. But despite the care he took to

ensure the Master's safety, Curtis experienced a
near-disaster halfway up Mount Carmel. After 'Abdu'l-Bahá
stepped out of the Cunningham and started walking down the
mountain, Curtis noticed the young Arab, who roared
around Haifa like a Grand Prix racer in competition, pushing
his car at top speed, heading for the Master. Alarm seized
Curtis. The speeding car missed the Master by inches.
'Abdu'l-Bahá never stopped walking, never flinched, turning
only to see who the driver was. It took Curtis a few moments
to regain his composure.

It didn't take long to unpack and arrange all of the parts of
the three lighting plants. But after that was taken care of,
Curtis found that he was running out of things to do. He
never liked sitting around doing nothing. He wasn't the
philosophical type who expends considerable energy trying
to prove his own existence, or reflecting on the origin of the
universe. He was a builder, a fairly creative builder who was
growing restless doing little odd jobs; and nothing had been
done to launch the lighting project. Fifteen days had passed
and there was still no word from the Master as to when he
would start. Curtis never mentioned his concern to
'Abdu'l-Bahá, for he knew that when He was ready to begin,
He would tell him. But Curtis was impatient; he was like an
anxious sprinter, crouched in the starting-block, waiting for
the signal to go. During some of his weaker moments, he
wondered about how long he would be in the Holy Land,
worrying about his obligation to his father's business. He had
to tell someone about his concern, and chose Rúhí Afnán, a
grandson of the Master.
    One day he and Rúhí were standing in the middle of the

street, about 150 feet from the door of 'Abdu'l-Bahá's house.

'Rúḥí,' he said, 'when do you think 'Abdu'l-Bahá is going to let me start the work on the lighting project?'

'I don't know ...'

Before Rúḥí could complete his response, the door to the Master's house swung open and 'Abdu'l-Bahá, in a booming voice, called out, 'We will start tomorrow.' He smiled, and walked back into the house. Though it was wonderful to hear the good news, Curtis was more impressed with the Master's power of knowing his very thoughts, his feelings. There was no way, he was convinced, that 'Abdu'l-Bahá could have heard his conversation with Rúḥí. After that experience, Curtis knew the Master knew him better than he knew himself. Who could explain the Mystery of God? Not Curtis, or anyone else.

That night Curtis learned that he was to accompany the Master to Bahjí the following day. Falling asleep was difficult; how could he sleep? For he had never been to the Shrine of Bahá'u'lláh, and he had never traveled with 'Abdu'l-Bahá outside of Haifa. The time passed so slowly. It must have been about 2 A.M. before exhaustion drew him into sleep. It was dawn when he opened his eyes. Standing in the doorway was the Master. Fujita and Luṭfu'lláh Ḥakím were awake also. Their immediate response was to sit up, but 'Abdu'l-Bahá urged them not to get out of bed, that they should rest. He turned to Curtis and said, 'I cannot go to Bahjí today to start the work; what shall I do about it?'

Curtis responded immediately: 'When the Master is ready I will be ready.'

'Balih! Balih!' (Yes! Yes!) said 'Abdu'l-Bahá – and left.

Though disappointed, Curtis didn't complain, because he

was certain there was a good reason why 'Abdu'l-Bahá wasn't going to Bahjí. He was amazed that he didn't want to indulge in self-pity, because back home such a disappointment would have hurt him deeply. But he knew he was in a special place, and he understood, without question, that the Master was a special figure who saw and heard things that others couldn't see or hear.

Several hours later, word reached Curtis that the Master was going to Bahjí, after all. Curtis was to be ready to leave by late afternoon. Somehow he knew that this time there would be no change in plans. So he rested well during the siesta. Before leaving, Curtis, Rúhí Afnán and a servant by the name of Khusraw gathered the food and tools, and put them into the high buckboard wagon. With the Master aboard, they headed for the railroad station, a sleepy little place where local Arabs liked to congregate with their camels. The train, filled with chattering people and their chickens and goats, was waiting for 'Abdu'l-Bahá and his party. But the Master sat down on a bench inside the station house. Outside, the conductor paced the platform. If the train arrived after sunset, the passengers would be unable to enter 'Akká, for the city closed its gates at nightfall. The conductor knew he couldn't leave without Sir 'Abdu'l-Bahá 'Abbás, who had come to the Holy Land as a prisoner and now was revered as 'The Father of the Poor.' It all seemed strange to Curtis; but he never questioned the wisdom of the situation. In about five minutes an Arab, leading his camel, approached, tied the animal to a post and entered the station house and headed for 'Abdu'l-Bahá. After a brief conversation, the Arab went his way and the Master boarded the train, which had windowless openings. Many passengers hung precariously out of the openings, but not because there wasn't enough room inside: they seemed to enjoy challenging the elements, much like those Americans who like riding the roller coaster. In the morning, the same train would be waiting to take most of the same people back to Haifa.

When the train pulled into 'Akká, the sun seemed to be sitting on the sea. It was cooler than when they had left Haifa, but not uncomfortable. Bahjí was two and a half miles from where they were. <u>Kh</u>usraw left immediately to prepare supper. All of the passengers rushed to 'Akká's gate, but 'Abdu'l-Bahá walked to the station house and sat down on a bench. Curtis and Rúḥí stood by patiently, with Curtis wondering what strange occurrence would unfold next. Only the howls of jackals could be heard, as night draped over 'Akká. In a few minutes, <u>Kh</u>alíd, a servant who lived in Bahjí, appeared with the Master's white donkey. Still, the Master remained seated. A full moon graced the night sky; and the stars sparkled the way they did over the Utah desert. It was so clear that Curtis could see in the distance an Arab, mounted on a white stallion, riding hard toward the station house. It was the person the Master was waiting for. They spoke for several minutes, laughing at times. Soon 'Abdu'l-Bahá emerged and mounted the donkey. The Arab headed back in the direction from which he had come, and was quickly enveloped by the night.

Walking to Bahjí that evening was one of the most memorable experiences in Curtis' life. Obviously, he was on Earth, but, in a sense, he wasn't, for he seemed detached from the tensions and woes of the world. Curtis never felt freer. His heart was filled with the vibrating love of 'Abdu'l-Bahá. It was a love that seemed to cleanse his inner being and move his spirit toward the wispy clouds that floated overhead. It didn't matter that nothing was said, for words were unnecessary. Who needed to say anything when you were immersed in peace and contentment? What wonderful things would happen next? Curtis thought.

After a while, the Master pulled His 'abá over his shoulders and spoke in English: 'Beautiful night, beautiful moon, beautiful clouds.' No one else commented. A moment or two later, 'Abdu'l-Bahá turned to Curtis, who was on His right, and said, 'Are you finding it difficult to walk?'

What could he say? Curtis thought. For in a sense he wasn't walking, rather, he was in the embrace of the Master.

'I am very happy to be walking with you,' he told 'Abdu'l-Bahá. If he had been more eloquent, he would have said what he really felt. But the Master knew why Curtis felt the way he did, for He said, 'You feel this way because you are filled with love.' At that point, Curtis could have floated.

When they reached Bahjí, they didn't go into the mansion because, at that time, it was held by the Covenant-breakers. Instead, they were to spend the night in a small building near the Shrine of Bahá'u'lláh. Its four rooms surrounded an open inner garden, with an orange-tree. In the dining room, Khusraw had spread out the dinner – a platter of small squash stuffed with rice, meat and candied orange-peel. There was a bowl of yogurt at each place, as well as a glass of tea, also a pitcher of sour milk and a large bowl with oranges, pomegranates and bunches of Damascus grapes.

The conversation was engaging, but not profound. In fact, most of the talk was about food, with 'Abdu'l-Bahá pointing out how tender the grapes were and how special the tea was. For Curtis the table-talk helped to pull him out of the state of heavenly intoxication. Around 'Abdu'l-Bahá people did useful things. Being enveloped in a mystical trance was not conducive to furthering an 'ever-advancing civilization.' 'Abdu'l-Bahá, Curtis knew, was the epitome of moderation. Even reading the Divine Word had its limits. A flight into spiritual realms shouldn't propel you away from the cares of the world, but should inspire you to be of service to others. Having been with the Master for nearly a month, Curtis discovered that He had a way of transporting you into those mystical realms and then gently leading you back to the world, which he considered a workshop where through serving others you sharpen and strengthen your character and draw closer to God.

About halfway through the meal, someone knocked on the outside door. 'Come in – in the name of God,' 'Abdu'l-Bahá called out in Arabic. When Khusraw finally removed the cross-bar and opened the door, there stood a tall Arab, about six-foot-three, with a black mustache and goatee. He didn't budge, until the Master said again, 'Come in – in the name of God.'

A chair was placed to the right of 'Abdu'l-Bahá, where the man was asked to sit. They engaged in an animated discussion, all in Arabic. At that point, the Master pushed His turban back on His head, and He and the man started laughing. Soon Rúhí began to laugh. It was contagious, because Curtis was swept up in the hilarity, even though he didn't understand a word that was uttered.

After the man left, Rúhí explained what had been discussed and what 'Abdu'l-Bahá had learned from the discussion. It seemed the Master had asked the Arab if he belonged to a tribe where the husband had to steal something during the day in order for his wife to allow him to enter their tent that night. When the man acknowledged that he belonged to such a tribe, the Master inquired if he had ever been denied entrance to the tent. 'Never,' the man declared. At that point 'Abdu'l-Bahá knew that the man sitting next to Him was the culprit who was stealing the sweet oranges in His garden in Bahjí. So the Master asked the man if he had ever tried eating sour oranges. When the Arab grimaced, 'Abdu'l-Bahá assured him that they tasted delicious with sugar. The next day 'Abdu'l-Bahá discovered that many of the sour oranges had been stripped from His trees.

At the World Center the day began at dawn and Curtis was awake at 5:20, eager to start work on the lighting project. After breakfast, the Master led him to the Shrine and selected the room where the lighting plant should be placed. During the rest of the morning, Curtis did some surveying work. But his eye caught more than the proportions of the Shrine's foundations. He realized how involved the Master was; that He was always serving, always putting the affairs of others ahead of His personal desires. Curtis had thought that 'Abdu'l-Bahá would find time to relax while at Bahjí, because Haifa was the center of the Bahá'í world; and Bahjí, he thought, was a refuge, where one would be cut off from the whirl and demands of civilization. But that was not the case. Somehow people who had needs found the Master; and when they appeared, He didn't show surprise – and never annoyance. Because of His attitude, those who came were calmed by Him, received assurance from Him, were fed by Him, felt appreciated and loved by Him and felt free to call upon Him again and again.

That morning several Arabs came from the countryside, seeking the Master. He fed them, gave them money, cheered their hearts. What He told them and Curtis, without saying so, was that He was their brother who would always be available in time of need. In the afternoon, the Governor of 'Akká called on the Master, spending several hours, seeking advice. Curtis felt that the Governor and many others in 'Akká, and elsewhere in Palestine, knew 'Abdu'l-Bahá's true authority. For He was the one who had answers to questions that others in high secular and ecclesiastical positions were unable to fathom.

At noontime, Curtis' spiritual longings were addressed by the Master, squeezing them in between the Arabs and the Governor. It was right after lunch while 'Abdu'l-Bahá was still at table, that Curtis approached Him, to share an experience that he could find no answer to. No person, however scholarly, could unravel the mystery. And how people tried, including his dear mother. 'What was that music?' he asked the Master, 'that enchanting music that permeated my room, while I was so sick in bed years ago in my parents' home, and cured me of typhoid fever?'

'It was a true spiritual experience. You heard music of the Kingdom,' 'Abdu'l-Bahá said, 'and it caused your spiritual awakening.'

The day they were to leave Bahjí, Curtis was up at five. Before breakfast he pumped enough water to shower the garden, then walked toward the house. The sun was barely up. Sitting on the porch was the Master, facing the sea. A plate full of jasmin blossoms was on a chair in front of Him. As Curtis approached the porch, he could smell the blossoms. It was like being in the Shrines, where floral fragrance was always present, and there was peace. 'Abdu'l-Bahá motioned to Curtis to sit beside Him, then poured Curtis a cup of tea.

'Did you sleep well?' Curtis asked.

The Master smiled and said in English, 'Last night I sleep very well.' Continuing to smile and looking at Curtis with a twinkle in His eye, He paused and then asked, 'Is my English good?'

'Yes,' Curtis responded. 'And I must learn Persian.'

'That would be very good.'

After that, nothing more was said. 'Abdu'l-Bahá and his American electrician watched the dawn chased away by the brilliance of golden daylight.

Later that morning, the Master asked Rúhí and Curtis to accompany Him to the Shrine of Bahá'u'lláh. Before entering, they removed their shoes. There was Curtis, tall, slender, open-faced, standing beside Rúhí and about three feet behind the Master at the threshold of the sepulcher that contained the bodily remains of the Blessed Beauty. Again, this simple young man from the West had been lifted into a heavenly state. Nothing but the pleading voice of 'Abdu'l-Bahá could be heard. Every other sound and thought vanished. Though he couldn't understand a word, Curtis was moved by the emotion of 'Abdu'l-Bahá chanting the Tablet of Visitation. There was no semblance of self from the figure before Curtis – just a total expression of devotion, a surrendering of will, an outpouring of love so intense that it seemed the Master was offering his heart to Bahá'u'lláh.

After prostrating before the Threshold for several minutes, 'Abdu'l-Bahá stood and asked Curtis and Rúhí to collect the rugs and ornaments in the Shrine, because they were to be taken to the House of 'Abbúd in 'Akká that afternoon. When that was done, the Master asked Curtis to come with Him. Curtis didn't wonder where they were going, or what was going to happen. That no longer mattered. What was real was the Master's request.

They walked in silence toward the Mansion. Halfway there, 'Abdu'l-Bahá stopped and asked Curtis how he planned to arrange the lighting of the Shrine of Bahjí. A surge of confidence swept over Curtis, and without hesitating, he explained that he would place underground lighting in the inner garden of the Shrine so that light would shine up through the flowers; that he would electrify the oil lamps, thus preserving their nineteenth-century character. And finally, he would place lights around the cornice of the Shrine. The Master nodded positively and exclaimed, 'Balih! Balih!'

As they walked closer to the Mansion, Curtis noticed an elderly man approach the Master. After introducing the believer to Curtis, 'Abdu'l-Bahá pointed out that the man, who was a mason, would help build the stone enclosure that was to house the lighting plant. The fact that the man didn't speak English and Curtis didn't know Persian or Arabic was never mentioned. It was understood that all would work out well. In 'Abdu'l-Bahá's mind, Curtis felt, the electrification project was done; it was only a matter of time before the world would appreciate the effort. The only thing that was necessary was the implementation of the plan.

When 'Abdu'l-Bahá and Curtis reached the small house where they had spent the night, they found the Master's four-seater high buckboard wagon standing at the entrance with Isfandíyár, the wagon's driver. All that had to go to 'Akká and Haifa was aboard.

They didn't go directly to the House of 'Abbúd, but stopped at the Most Great Prison, where 'Abdu'l-Bahá had spent two years. Nothing extraordinary occurred; 'Abdu'l-Bahá simply gazed at the massive sandstone structure. In His silence, He seemed to say to Curtis that only a few people in the world knew that this foul place was where a divine Manifestation of God was sent to perish.

The House of 'Abbúd was only a few minutes' ride from the prison. Inside, the dining-room table was set, with three extra places. Minutes after 'Abdu'l-Bahá had arrived, the guests appeared. Three Druzes, including the chief of those people and his two sons, showed up for dinner, obviously invited by the Master, who greeted them warmly. The chief, in his nineties, did most of the speaking during the dinner and afterwards. Curtis sensed that the man, who respected and loved 'Abdu'l-Bahá, was distressed. Speaking in a pleading voice, expressing puzzlement, and at times weeping, the chief searched 'Abdu'l-Bahá's face for some assurance.

The Master said little – simply trying to comfort the old man, patting his back from time to time.

Several months later Curtis understood why the Druze chief was so depressed. He probably sensed that he would never see 'Abdu'l-Bahá again, his adviser, his comforter, his friend, his wise counselor, and in a sense, his spiritual father. The Master's trip to Bahjí with Curtis was His last visit there: about a month later 'Abdu'l-Bahá passed away. The Druzes, a religious sect, shun serious association with outsiders. But they considered 'Abdu'l-Bahá an honored member of the community, a rare distinction. They grieved deeply over the Master's passing.

After dinner, Curtis, Rúhí and Isfandíyár packed the

buckboard wagon again and the Master led them back to Haifa via a road along the sea. It was a delightful journey. Nature seemed to soothe the senses, burying the experience of the weeping Druze chieftain deep in Curtis' memory, far from his conscious mind. Halfway back, they noticed a magnificent sunset over Mount Carmel. They stopped so Curtis could snap a picture of it. A few minutes later it was night-time. The reflection of the moon on the sea, the clusters of stars, the balmy night, the nearness of the Master were a symphony that drove every care away. Curtis didn't notice how long it took to reach Haifa; he didn't care that 'Abdu'l-Bahá didn't utter a word all the way. He and Rúhí sat behind the Master, who was behind the driver. Curtis focused on 'Abdu'l-Bahá's back, noticing how His long white hair fell over his shoulders. Curtis never felt more secure.

Only years after his experiences with 'Abdu'l-Bahá was Curtis able to fully appreciate the tranquil and happy atmosphere at the World Center. Almost every day there was laughter. Racial and cultural prejudice was nonexistent. Persian, Arab, Japanese and American mingled naturally. No issue – pro or con – was made over someone's ethnic background. It was completely understood that all humans were part of the same family, God's family. And there was never any complaining, no sarcasm, no expressions of negativity. Backbiting wasn't experienced. And that was remarkable considering the turbulence and intrigue that swirled around the Master. The Covenant-breakers were in His midst, always plotting against Him, trying to embarrass Him before the governmental authorities and scheming to seize all of the Holy properties; and they were in control of the Bahjí Mansion, neglecting to repair what would break or

ABOVE: Curtis and Ḥusayn on their way to Bahjí, 1921. BELOW Curtis and Lutfu'lláh Ḥakím in their Haifa living quarters, 1921.

TOP: Curtis eating lunch at Bahjí, 1921.
BOTTOM: Curtis sitting on the Master's donkey, 1921.

ABOVE: The Master aboard
His buckboard wagon, 1921.
RIGHT: Fujita in 1921, near
the Master's house. He liked
dressing in Persian attire.

ABOVE AND BELOW: Two views of the lighting generators that Curtis installed on Mount Carmel. TOP RIGHT: First electric lights installed in Haifa by Curtis, 1922. BOTTOM RIGHT: Curtis sitting on the steps of the Bahjí Pilgrim House, 1921.

K. Lolel
Sayyid Abdul Qasem   } on the steps of the
Mirza   Pilgrim Hous...

S. Oct. 19. 1921 Bahji

ABOVE: 'Abdu'l-Bahá's coffin being carried out of His house. BELOW: The crowd listening to dignitaries speaking at 'Abdu'l-Bahá's funeral. Both photographs believed to have been taken by Curtis.

stop functioning. There was always news of the believers being persecuted in Persia and elsewhere, and outbreaks of discord in the fledgling Bahá'í communities around the world. There was the daily pressure of guiding the infant Faith, nurturing it in such a way that the believers wouldn't lose heart, or feel so unworthy of being able to live by the Bahá'í standard that they withered into apathy. Every day He would write letters, scores of letters, usually answering correspondence He had received from Bahá'ís around the planet; and no subject was avoided, however silly it might appear on the surface. People in the Holy Land, Jew, Christian, Druze and Muslim, often clergymen, sought Him out for advice. While carrying the weight of the world, with all of its open wounds, He managed to tend to the sick and poor in the Haifa area and be a concerned husband and father.

Though Curtis experienced tranquillity and happiness in Haifa, people worked and worked hard. The Abhá Kingdom, he reflected later in life, must be like the World Center as it was while the Master lived there. It certainly wasn't an isolated sanctuary where people floated about in pleated white gowns, perpetually smiling and strumming miniature harps. People had chores, and they believed that what they were doing was helping, in a small way, to create a brighter future, to build that world civilization that Bahá'u'lláh shares with us through His revelation. They worked – but without complaining, backbiting, gossip and negativity; no cheating, lying and scheming for power. For Curtis it was that atmosphere that made the World Center Heaven on Earth. While in Haifa, Curtis felt everything Bahá'u'lláh called for was attainable; that in time, if the believers put into practice what He urged them to do, they would be able to remake the world as He envisioned it would be. Back in America it seemed more difficult to maintain that perspective. There were so many distractions. But it could be done by developing a dependence upon the Revelation for guidance in every aspect of life. That's what Curtis – after many tests and failures – eventually learned to do.

To Curtis the World Center was light, constantly flowing; and 'Abdu'l-Bahá generated it. It was easier to be happy there. In fact, while he was there, Curtis never thought about happiness because he was experiencing it. It was like the fish who was oblivious of water, because he was always immersed in it. The Master was happy despite the troubles and problems He faced, because He understood the day in which He lived. Bahá'u'lláh was pointing the way. So the Master followed and rejoiced, and those near Him in spirit also rejoiced.

Chapter 5

It was the dream of the Master to have the Shrine of the Báb bathed in light and at the same time to look across the Bay of Haifa and see the Shrine of Bahá'u'lláh illumined. In order to be able to do this, He told Curtis, 'You are to spend two weeks working in Bahjí, then return to Haifa to work on the Shrine of the Báb for two weeks – and you are to follow this pattern until you have completed your work.'

After Curtis acknowledged the procedure, 'Abdu'l-Bahá introduced him to a young Persian who had come from India. He was Ḥusayn-i-Kahrubáyí, the electrician who had appeared in Haifa a year earlier, volunteering to install the three lighting plants, but was sent home and was asked to wait until the Master called him. 'Abdu'l-Bahá told Curtis that Ḥusayn was going to help him, and assured him that they would learn to work well together even though they could not understand each other's language. Of course working with someone you couldn't understand would be considered unorthodox back home, and in some quarters downright foolish. In putting together a work crew, Curtis was always taught, you make sure you select people who will work well together, people who will complement each other and be able to communicate easily. A good combination of people will assure effective, fast results. But in Haifa, Curtis had to scrap some of his management training, because he wasn't working for an executive in the Woolworth Building. 'Abdu'l-Bahá had special ways. And Curtis knew that. In time, he felt, the wisdom of his working with Husayn would become clear.

So both men tried valiantly to overcome their differences, concentrating on ways to communicate. First they discovered they had a limited vocabulary of each other's language. For example, Curtis knew words like balih ('yes'), inshá'lláh ('if God will') and marhabá ('Well done!' or 'Welcome!'); and Husayn knew a few terms like 'okay,' 'all right' and 'good.' With a combination of the words they knew, a series of facial expressions and hand gestures, they were able to devise a system by which to work efficiently together. Before starting the actual work, they laid all of their tools out on a large table. When Curtis held up a tool, he would call out its English name and Husayn would give the Persian name. They employed the same method with the lighting plant parts. It didn't take long before they at least had a basic knowledge of the working nomenclature. Certainly this arrangement would never have been tolerated by Curtis' father. But it worked, despite the strange grunting, peppered with words like 'balih' and 'okay' and exaggerated facial expressions and hand gestures. An objective Western observer watching the way the American and Persian were working together would probably have thought he was witnessing a rehearsal of some theatrical comedy production. But all went well. From this experience, Curtis realized that people of different cultures, who don't speak the same language, can learn to understand each other, even learn to like each other. What's necessary is a willingness to try, to view the other person as your equal, have a positive attitude, and faith that it will work out. Of course, Curtis never forgot that it was 'Abdu'l-Bahá who made it possible for him to gain insight into how humanity can be united.

For the next ten days Curtis spent time exploring the area around the Shrine of the Báb for a site to install the lighting plant and sketched out how he was going to wire the Holy Tomb. Time was also spent purchasing pipe and other supplies in town. On Sundays 'Abdu'l-Bahá would gather with the friends at the Shrine of the Báb. Curtis always liked being there, not only because the Master would speak on some aspect of the Faith, but also because he especially looked forward to 'Abdu'l-Bahá holding his hand and placing rose water in his palm. It was something He did to all of the believers before they entered the Shrine.

On the Sunday he was to go to Bahjí to start the actual physical work, Curtis and Luṭfu'lláh were in town purchasing materials. Curtis wasn't going to miss being with the Master, not since he was going to be away from Him for two weeks. Every moment with Him was a feast for his soul. So Curtis made sure they got back in time for the meeting. About fifty believers were there. What impressed Curtis most that sunny afternoon was the walk down the mountain, with the Master in the lead. It was a heavenly processional. He could have followed the Master into the sea, if that was where He wished to go. Strange, but it was only 'Abdu'l-Bahá and the Faith that could command such obedience of a young man who had continually battled with authority throughout his life.

Suddenly, 'Abdu'l-Bahá turned around and said He had some business to attend to and proceeded down the steep rocky side of the mountain, moving quickly. No one knew exactly where He was going; but He had done the same thing before whenever He felt someone in town was in terrible need.

October 28 marked a month that Curtis had been at the World Center. As usual, he got up at five, washed and went to the shop to fix a gas torch. He had been there only a few minutes when 'Abdu'l-Bahá appeared, saying 'Good morning my son, good morning my son. How are you?'

What a way to be greeted in the morning, Curtis thought – the Center of the Covenant looking at you so lovingly. No one else ever looked at him that way, not even his mother. It was an outpouring that penetrated every fiber of his being.

Curtis asked if he, Ḥusayn and Luṭfu'lláh could go to Bahjí that day to begin the actual work.

'Very good,' responded the Master.

Since the train to 'Akká didn't leave until late in the afternoon, Curtis remained in the garage putting things in order and packing. 'Abdu'l-Bahá's room was close to the garage, and while Curtis worked,'he could hear the Master dictating a very long tablet.

The thought of starting to install the lighting plants thrilled Curtis, but the fact that he would be in Bahjí, away from the Master for two weeks, concerned him. How frustrating – knowing that 'Abdu'l-Bahá was about fifteen miles away in Haifa and being unable to be with Him, watch Him, listen to Him. But Curtis' fear never came to pass. He went to Bahjí all right, but somehow – maybe through a subconscious drive of his – he found a reason to return to Haifa from time to time, to pick up materials he needed for his work. Every time he came back, he would see or speak to the Master. Not for long, just for a few seconds. But that was enough for Curtis. One time, however, he met 'Abdu'l-Bahá in front of His home, and asked Him something he had wanted to ask for weeks but couldn't find the courage to: Curtis asked if he could take the Ford to Bahjí, so that if he had to return to Haifa to pick up supplies he wouldn't have to rely on the shaky railroad schedule.

Curtis was granted his wish, but he didn't abuse it. He returned to Haifa only about four or five times. Meanwhile, much was accomplished at Bahjí. It was a spartan life – up at five, prayers, a couple of hours of work, breakfast, more work, lunch, a nap, more work, supper and more work, and at times reflection near the Tomb of Bahá'u'lláh.

Washing one's body was done before supper, close to sunset. Right after work Luṭfu'lláh and Curtis would rush to the old stone viaduct, wash their clothes in the cold, clear water, then take a bath Bahjí-style: Curtis would strip nude and stand on a boulder and Luṭfu'lláh would cast buckets of cold water on him; then Curtis would wash Luṭfu'lláh down.

Curtis, Luṭfu'lláh and Ḥusayn lived in the cottage where the Master stayed when He visited Bahjí. And they ate well. The Master made sure of that. He was especially conscious of Curtis' food needs, because they were different from Ḥusayn's. He made certain that Curtis received enough protein, something he sensed most Americans craved. Spending nine months in the United States and Canada, the Master gained a deep understanding of American customs and tastes. Normally, people in the Middle East do not eat

eggs in the morning; but the Master made sure the young
American had them for breakfast. In a note to the caretaker
at Bahjí, 'Abdu'l-Bahá urged him to feed Curtis well:

> He is God!
> To Áqá Siyyid Abu'l-Qásim:
> A dear guest is coming to you; he is the person who is going to
> arrange the lighting of the Holy Shrines with Mr Kahrabá'í. He
> must have plentiful food for lunch and dinner, and even breakfast.
> Therefore a quantity of jam, cheese and olives will be sent and Mr
> Luṭfu'lláh, who knows a little about cooking, will accompany him.
> You must all do what you can to ensure that at lunch and dinner
> there will be at least one type of dish that is to his liking. Either kill a
> chicken or bring meat from 'Akká. There must always be some kind
> of meat. And in the morning, serve milk, eggs, jam and olives. It
> will be some trouble for you but this service is the duty of
> 'Abdu'l-Bahá. I should be doing this but have no opportunity and
> so you must make the effort. Upon thee be the Glory of Glories.
>
> 'Abdu'l-Bahá 'Abbás

After two weeks, Curtis was back in Haifa, close to the
Master again. For some reason the Master never came up to
inspect the work that Ḥusayn and he had done in Bahjí. To
demonstrate such trust amazed Curtis. Every boss he had
ever worked for was usually hanging over his shoulder. But
the World Center was a different place, operating on
different principles. 'Abdu'l-Bahá's concern was not that the
work wasn't going to be done well, but that Curtis and
Ḥusayn had all of the supplies they needed. Curtis sensed
that the Master had already envisioned the project
completed; that all that was necessary was the implementation of the plan, which was mechanical. What He saw
in the world of the spirit, where He dwelt, were the two

Shrines aglow in the evening. He had assembled all of the necessary ingredients to make tangible what He already saw. With God's help, it would all materialize.

One of the blessings of being in Haifa was having lunch with the Master every day. 'Abdu'l-Bahá insisted that Curtis eat with Him. One day Curtis was late coming to lunch, because he had to wash and change clothes. He wouldn't ever sit down at the luncheon table with the Master in his overalls. 'Abdu'l-Bahá had other ideas about that. He told Curtis that there was no need for him to change his work clothes.

Eating lunch with 'Abdu'l-Bahá generated feelings that, on the surface, wouldn't be considered compatible. For example, Curtis sensed the Master's majesty; but he felt completely at ease with Him, while normally, most people who find themselves close to nobility are restrained, extremely self-conscious, or ill at ease. After the meal, 'Abdu'l-Bahá would remain at the table, at times talking about the struggles and sacrifices of the early believers. Other times he would sit quietly reading mail or papers, often pushing His turban back on his head, completely absorbed in what He was doing. Curtis enjoyed just sitting and watching, observing all this. The simple experience evoked a sense of peace in Curtis, for which he had no explanation.

Often only Curtis and Fujita would be together at the table; and they had their favorite games. One involved the Master's brown cat. Fujita, who took care of the cat for 'Abdu'l-Bahá, would always lock the cat in the kitchen during lunch. He did that just to hear the Master say, 'Let the cat out,' which, of course, Fujita would do. As soon as the kitchen door was opened, the cat would dart to the feet of 'Abdu'l-Bahá, who would stroke her and feed her. After gobbling the food, the cat would brush against the Master's feet and purr loudly. Everyone knew it was a joke, but it was fun for all. It was amazing to Curtis that the 'Mystery of God' would derive such pleasure from such simple things. On the one hand He was so human, in the best sense of the term, and yet Curtis knew from personal experience that 'Abdu'l-Bahá possessed powers no one else had. What made the Master so appealing was His naturalness, His openness, His genuine concern for you.

'Abdu'l-Bahá had mothering qualities, which He openly displayed, and they were usually demonstrated to Curtis at lunch. When Curtis took a helping of whatever was on the table, 'Abdu'l-Bahá would invariably say, 'Take more. You are a young man, so you should eat much.' It was something he would expect from his mother, but not his father.

One afternoon after the cat had been patted and fed by the Master, Curtis asked what the difference was between the life of a cat and a human being. 'Abdu'l-Bahá's response was difficult to comprehend. He gave a discourse on the ingestion and digestion of what we eat, being extremely detailed in explaining the various processes involved, and pointing out that what is of value nourishes the body and what is not is eliminated as waste. Then He arose, walking across the floor. As His foot struck a loose tile, He stopped, looked at it and exclaimed: 'It is progressing, and it is possible for it to reach the state of a mirror.' Years later, after deepening in the Teachings, Curtis gained some insight into the Master's explanation when he read in the Writings: 'We have placed mankind in the alembic, and after due refining processes, the believers are the fragrant extracts thereof.'

Chapter 6

Meticulous about his work, Curtis didn't want to do anything that would flaw the lighting project in any way. Even aesthetic matters concerned him. The thought of having to lay the thick black wire, that Roy sent over, along the Shrines' interior walls, bothered him. The wires should be buried behind the walls. Special wiring was needed, and the only place where he could secure it was in Cairo.

'Abdu'l-Bahá gave Curtis $600 and asked that he take Fujita along because 'he would enjoy Cairo.' The Master loved Fujita dearly, showering special care over the precious pearl from Japan. Every day the two would have breakfast together – alone. It was a time of peace, when the Master could bask in the light of Fujita's purity, not having to meet any demands. Often their breakfasts were feasts of laughter, especially after 'Abdu'l-Bahá asked Fujita to grow a beard. When full-grown, it was at best a thin collection of long hairs, nothing like the thick luxuriant beards Persians grow. The Master enjoyed stroking Fujita's wispy beard, usually making Him laugh. Fujita was happy that he could bring pleasure to 'Abdu'l-Bahá's life. But there was a time when he questioned whether he could be doing something more useful than serving 'Abdu'l-Bahá.

Fujita, who came from a prominent Japanese family, heard of the Faith in San Francisco from Mrs Helen Goodall. Before becoming a Bahá'í, he was a notorious party-hopper, associating with theater people. Learning that Fujita had become a Bahá'í, the Master wrote him a tablet, praising him for the step he had taken and for the wonderful person he was. 'The person He's writing about,' Fujita thought, 'couldn't be me.' So he didn't take the letter seriously. After the third letter from 'Abdu'l-Bahá, Fujita wrote the Master asking what he could do to best serve the Faith. 'Go back to school,' 'Abdu'l-Bahá advised. Fujita went to Ann Arbor, Michigan to study.

In 1912 Fujita met the Master, who urged him to complete his schooling. Upon graduation, 'Abdu'l-Bahá promised, He would have him come to the World Center to work. Fujita went to Chicago to complete his engineering studies. He spent seven years, living with Mrs Corinne True and her family. Afterwards he went to Haifa, but never got close to a drafting table. He found himself working as a servant in the Western Pilgrim House, certainly not putting into practice what he had studied at the university. This disturbed him; being in Haifa, he convinced himself, was a mistake, and he decided to go back to America. While packing his clothes, Rúhí Afnán appeared, stating that 'Abdu'l-Bahá wanted to see him immediately. Fujita ran to the Master's house. As he entered 'Abdu'l-Bahá's room, the Master said, 'What is the matter, Fujita?'

'You told me to study certain things, and I'm not doing them here.'

'Fujita,' the Master said, 'if I wanted a mechanic or engineer I could have gotten one easily. The work you are doing for me is what 'Abdu'l-Bahá wishes you to do.'

The Master's love dispelled every trace of self-pity and Fujita replied, 'If I must shine the Master's shoes that would be fine for me.' Fujita had gained understanding: he was a servant of the Servant of Glory. What greater honor could there be? For there was no greater station in this life than servitude.

Curtis and Fujita together must have generated stares from passers-by. Fujita in his shoes was less than five foot tall, possessing what Curtis called a 'wispy, moth-eaten beard.' Curtis on the other hand was about six foot, rangy, and took long strides when he walked. Half the time Fujita had to trot to keep up with Curtis. Though superficially different, they grew to like each other, often swimming together in the sea on hot days and sharing some of their deepest thoughts and feelings.

Excited that he was going to Cairo, Fujita insisted on taking his tuxedo along, which he vowed he would wear. Curtis was skeptical about Fujita's chances of wearing it, because they were on a purchasing mission, and they had not received invitations to any balls.

It was dark when they arrived in Cairo. While standing on the platform of the Cairo railroad station, wondering what hotel they should go to, they heard a woman call, 'Alláh-u-Abhá.' They turned and saw a large woman, dressed in fancy clothes, followed by her two sons and a daughter. This American lady had met Curtis and Fujita while on pilgrimage, and when she approached them, asked, 'What brings you to Cairo?'

When they explained, she insisted that they stay where she was staying – the Continental Hotel, one of the most expensive hotels in northern Africa in 1921.

As they stepped into the lobby, they were dazzled by the elegance of the place. Every person seemed so self-assured, so important. And because Curtis and Fujita were there, the hotel-workers assumed that they were people of high social rank. The bell-hop who escorted them to their room treated them with deference. But that illusion was soon shattered when they reached the room. When the bell-hop opened the door, both Curtis and Fujita gaped at the opulence before them. What a contrast to their room in Haifa. Fujita wasn't one to hide his feelings; he dropped his suitcase and sprinted to one of the two large beds and dove onto one of them. Curtis burst into laughter, because there was Fujita enveloped by the thick quilts, with only his face exposed, beaming with delight, enjoying thoroughly something he had taken for granted during his party-hopping days in California.

For a few minutes both men acted as if they had been dispatched to some dream world, because they had difficulty believing that their new surroundings were real. They had just come from a place where the mattresses were only three-quarters of an inch thick, and you shook out your shoes before putting them on lest your toes be greeted by a scorpion.

The beds were so soft, so appealing that the first thing they decided to do was sleep and sleep for as long as they wanted. But that plan was quickly altered, because soon after making their decision, they heard someone knocking on the door. It was a bell-hop, dressed in a colorful uniform, with a message from the lady who had invited them to stay at the Continental Hotel. 'Would you please join me for dinner?' she asked. Fujita wasn't yawning anymore; the message had infused new energy into him. Curtis watched what he thought would never materialize actually happen. Fujita tore into his suitcase, pulled out his tuxedo and put it on. Somehow, Curtis felt, 'Abdu'l-Bahá had made it possible for Fujita to carry out his wish.

When they reached the lobby, Fujita seemed to take charge, walking ahead of Curtis and the lady who had invited them to dinner, his tuxedo tails almost touching the rich oriental rugs. As he approached the dining room, one of the hotel's elegantly dressed butlers, standing erect, opened the thick oak doors. It was a majestic entry. The only thing missing was a series of trumpet fanfares and the roll of the drum. Terribly self-conscious, Curtis walked down the aisle after Fujita, who was bowing to the left and then to the right. The men on both sides stood and bowed back, sensing that Fujita was some sort of royal figure from the orient.

No sooner had they been seated, than a butler approached Fujita and whispered something in his ear. Fujita arose and proceeded to the door, again bowing to the left and then the right, the gentlemen on both sides responding in kind.

As Fujita entered the lobby, he was greeted by a large Persian who swept him into his arms and kissed his beard. The Persian had heard from pilgrims that the Master enjoyed stroking Fujita's beard.

The trip to Cairo was successful. Curtis purchased the wire he needed, and his dear friend Fujita was able to satisfy a long yearning. After the Cairo episode, Fujita stopped opening his trunk to show off his rich collection of clothing to Curtis and Luṭfu'lláh. It was as if the experience in Egypt had severed a certain attachment that Fujita had had to the old status quo.

In the United States, Curtis would never think of going to a place to hear someone speak, if the speaker spoke in a language he couldn't understand. But in Haifa Curtis wouldn't miss 'Abdu'l-Bahá's talks in the Pilgrim House every night, or on Sunday in the central front room of the Shrine of the Báb. The Master spoke in either Arabic or Persian. Yet Curtis was drawn to the meetings by 'Abdu'l-Bahá; and he sat like the other people with his arms folded across his chest, at times wearing a fez. Not that that was a special way that Bahá'ís were to sit in the presence of the Master. It was simply something the local people did whenever they sat before someone they deemed prominent or revered. So that he wouldn't insult or slight them, this young American, who had the spirit of a cowboy, struggled to adopt the local people's customs.

The Master must have known that Curtis' intentions were pure and that he was gaining something by attending the meetings. One evening, about midway through His talk, 'Abdu'l-Bahá looked over at Curtis and asked in English, 'Do you understand what is being said here?'

'No, Master,' Curtis responded. 'I do not speak the languages.'

'Well, your heart understands, and the language of the heart is much stronger than the language of words.'

After that experience, Curtis began to understand that words weren't required to reach true communication with someone. As his understanding of that experience grew, he was able to be with someone and feel comfortable without uttering a word. He also learned from 'Abdu'l-Bahá that a pure expression of love can settle a troubled heart, even answer questions that one is afraid to ask openly. Curtis experienced this one Sunday while in the Shrine of the Báb, attending a talk by the Master. He found his mind drifting and questioning various aspects of the Teachings, which he didn't understand. It was troubling him. While his eyes were focused on the floor, Curtis felt a strong impulse to look up. When he did, he noticed the Master in the far corner looking at him and smiling. Though nothing was said, all of Curtis' questions and doubts vanished.

In a way Curtis' experience in the Holy Land with 'Abdu'l-Bahá was an ongoing lesson on how to live life. Everything that happened was meaningful, even death, especially how we die.

Elderly Abu'l-Ḥasan, who belonged to the family of the Báb, committed suicide at dawn one day. He didn't take his life because he felt he was a drain on his family and 'Abdu'l Bahá: he was an able workman at the World Center and the Master loved him dearly. Nor was it because he had suffered so much in his life, especially in Persia. His suicide was a carefully calculated act. After settling all of his personal affairs, he strode down to the sea, folded his clothes neatly, and leaving them on the beach, walked into the sea. His death grieved 'Abdu'l-Bahá. On the day of the funeral, the Master helped to carry Abu'l-Ḥasan's coffin to the grave site.

Curtis learned from 'Abdu'l-Bahá that there was no valid reason for committing suicide. That point was made in addressing the friends in His nightly talk at His home, the day after Abu'l-Ḥasan's funeral.

'No one should injure himself on purpose or take his own life,' He said; 'God never places a burden on us greater than we can carry. Each burden we endure is for our own good and development. Should anyone at any time encounter hard and perplexing times, he must say to himself, "This too will pass;" then he will grow calm.

'When experiencing difficulties,' He added, 'I would say to myself "this too will pass away," and I would become calm again.'

'Now if someone cannot be patient and endure then it is better for him to arise in the service of the Cause of God. It would be better for him to pursue the path of martyrdom than to commit suicide.'

A few days after making those statements, 'Abdu'l-Bahá passed away, ending a lifetime of martyrdom. The friends then realized that Mírzá Abu'l-Ḥasan had sensed that the one he loved more than anyone else would soon be gone and that he couldn't bear to live without Him.

Chapter 7

Valeria Kelsey longed to receive a letter from her son. So much time passed between letters. She knew he was busy helping the Master, that there was little spare time and very little energy left for writing letters after a dawn-to-dusk work day. But understanding the reason for not writing didn't remove the ache in her heart. How she wanted to know what the Master was like, what insights He had shared with Curtis regarding the application of the Faith in meeting life's mounting challenges. She wanted to know how 'Abdu'l-Bahá spent His day; the way He steered the ship of the Cause through the wild waters of the world. How she wished she could stand at the foot of Mount Carmel and gaze at the resting place of the Báb, bow her head before the threshold of the Tomb of Bahá'u'lláh and sit with 'Abdu'l-Bahá, knowing she could hide nothing from Him, and not caring that He knew her deepest secrets. 'Abdu'l-Bahá was the only one on Earth in whom she had total trust. She had no doubts as to what He represented to humanity. It was frustrating to have someone so close to her – dear Curtis, her only human link with the Master – and not be able to share his feelings, thoughts and insights about the World Center, a place she knew was her real home. How she wanted to know more about it, to be drawn into its soul-cleansing spirit, to surrender to her Lord.

Checking the mailbox was one of the most exciting moments of her day; it was also the most disappointing when there was no letter from Curtis. But Valeria had experienced disappointment before – lots of it; and she knew adversity, even as a child. She never knew her father; her mother's parents, living in Missouri, came to her house one day while her father was away working and whisked her and their daughter from their home in Carthage, Illinois. Valeria was eighteen months old when the abduction took place. Every attempt by her father to reclaim his family, even communicate with them, was rebuffed. For years she searched for her father. In 1904, married and a mother, and living in Salt Lake City, she discovered that he was living in Ottumwa, Iowa, as a Methodist minister. She yearned to see him – but never did, for he died shortly after he answered her letter:

'If the past years have made you hungry to see me, to know me, to hear from me, think how this old heart of mine would bound with joy to kiss the lips of a daughter that was sweet to me in babyhood. All the long, long years of the past I have prayed to God to open your heart to a hungry father's love. Now see how your letter comes like opening buds of spring with expectations of untold joy ...'

In marriage, Valeria experienced tragedy: her son, Allen, bright, sweet and radiant, was stricken by scarlet fever and died at the age of fourteen; a daughter, Katherine, born with a hole in her spine, lived for only an hour. Valeria asked Curtis to pray for his brother and sister at the Shrines.

And living with a man who didn't share the most meaningful thing in her life, her religion, was an agony she had to endure for fifteen years. How she yearned for him to embrace what she had embraced, for she loved him, despite his puritanical ways and volcanic temper. He was honest, genuine, hard-working, thoughtful, a man of outstanding integrity, who cared deeply for his family; but he viewed the Faith as an intrusion into his family's life. He was suspicious of all organizations, especially religions. He tried hard to be tolerant, but his hostility would explode in fits of temper from time to time. Three members of his family swept up in some strange Eastern religion! The energy and time they spent for the Faith, he felt, could have been channeled into developing a happier, more united family. Valeria knew how he felt, even though he rarely talked about his feelings. He was the kind of person who kept his troubles to himself. Every attempt by Valeria to unlock his heart so the light of the spirit could touch it was beaten back by him. As the years passed he drew further and further away from the outstretched arms of his wife, never realizing what he was doing. That was the source of deep grief for Valeria.

Roy Wilhelm sensed Valeria's yearning for a letter from Curtis. So as soon as he received correspondence from the Master referring to Curtis, he extracted the reference and sent it to her, thinking it would cheer her heart:

'The electrician, Mr Kelsey, arrived. He is a real man. Really, that dear friend is confirmed with utmost energy in the service of the Cause of God. This is from the Heavenly blessings.'

Valeria couldn't help feeling proud of her son after reading and rereading and studying those few sentences by 'Abdu'l-Bahá. The Master knew Curtis' essence – she was certain of that. His penetrative sight had explored her son's reality. For the rest of her life Valeria valued that short communiqué as one of her most prized possessions.

But what Roy had hoped for wasn't really accomplished. His note only intensified Valeria's longing to know from Curtis the ways of the Master, and how he interacted with Him.

The first letter Valeria received from Curtis was post-marked Naples. In it, Curtis described the hunch he had about going from France to Naples, to try to gain passage on any ship heading for Alexandria. Valeria was impressed with Curtis' ability to follow his intuition. It was also a sign that 'Abdu'l-Bahá was guiding Curtis to the Holy Land. That put her mind at rest regarding his physical well-being; Curtis was being protected.

After the Naples letter there was not even a note from him until November 26, 1921 – only a cablegram stating that he had arrived safely in Haifa.

Valeria wrote Curtis faithfully, one or two letters a week. She never complained about the infrequency of his letters; but she did reveal how much she missed him and yearned to hear from him, never degenerating into bitterness or self pity – more like a lonely heart asking to be embraced.

The happiest sections of her letters dealt with successes she and other Bahá'ís had had in teaching. The prospect of being able to teach someone brought her happiness: 'It seems there is a Jewish man who comes to Mrs Watson's (a non-Bahá'í) house once a week, who is a collector; and he is very intelligent. She got to talking to him, telling him about me, that she had met a woman who had no race prejudice and who was a Mohammadan (Isn't that too funny?). He asked her a lot of questions as to what the teachings were, and he became greatly interested. Then she showed him the letters, with 'Abdu'l-Bahá's name on the envelope, and he put his hand to his face and cried out, "That proves it, that proves it!" Just what it proved to him I do not know, but anyway, he wants to come to see me and find out more about the Revelation ... It is always so thrilling to see the way the spirit works ...'

Fortunately, Valeria had a lot to do while Curtis was away and that kept her from dwelling on Curtis all of the time. But she couldn't drive him completely out of mind. There was always an undercurrent of concern, more pronounced when she was idle.

The Kelseys' move to the heart of Manhattan, West 77th Street, took up lots of her time and energy. In many ways it was better living in the city: Frank was closer to his office, and Valeria was in the center of Bahá'í activity. She enjoyed attending the Kinneys' weekly fireside: and there were so many people to teach about the Faith. The city was full of men and women searching for meaning in life, people who had stripped themselves of provincial ideas and attitudes and were seeking something new and vital in which to believe. And Feasts were accessible. In the city Valeria seemed close to the Master, because messages from the World Center came to Roy's office in Wall Street; and the latest news about the Master was circulated in New York City before anywhere else.

But there were things about the city she didn't like – the

lack of natural growth was one thing. She preferred the blossoms of a fruit tree to the towering collection of bricks and glass, standing forty stories high. A city park was not like an open meadow or forest where a person is encompassed by nature's beauty. Strolling in Central Park was like touring one of the city's museums, where you gawked at the trees and flowers as if they were strange artifacts from a distant land or an ancient culture.

Deep down Valeria knew that without Bahá'u'lláh and 'Abdu'l-Bahá she would be consumed with unhappiness, for life at home was trying. This was apparent in her letters to Curtis. It wasn't something she expressed directly: 'October is gone, and we have not seen the hills or the color on the trees! But God's Glory is everywhere, and what if the phases of Nature's beauty fade? It comes again with greater loveliness than ever – and always will this be. I love to think of the silent earth in the winter time, under its blanket of snow and ice. Who knows what alchemy goes on there? Only when spring comes do we get a small idea. And so it is with man in the cold and ice of sorrow and hardship; He is preparing his season of greater expression in the Glory of God.'

Valeria was busy writing. *Reality* magazine published her poem on the Italian tenor, Enrico Caruso, and an article on disarmament; and she was making headway in editing her novel *The Immortal Cup*, which a New York publisher was planning to publish; and time was spent in polishing her play, *The Fountain*.

There were domestic problems that required her time, energy and prayers while Curtis was away. Arthur, her eldest son, seemed lost in the world, unable to hold a job, a source of irritation to his father. Though a Bahá'í, he spent more time drafting astrological charts than deepening in the Faith. The several attempts he made to work for his father failed. Arthur's ways disturbed his father and the two argued frequently. Often Valeria found herself refereeing their battles. It got so bad that Arthur would come home only when he knew his father was away on business. When Arthur was with his mother, he seemed genuinely interested in the Bahá'í Writings and would leave feeling enthusiastic about the Faith, promising to stay close to the Teachings. But on his own, he would drift back to astrology. In her letters to Curtis, she often urged him to pray for Arthur and asked Curtis to seek guidance from 'Abdu'l-Bahá on how to help her eldest son. She knew Arthur had considerable potential and that he was frustrated because he seemed thwarted in developing it. He was gifted in mathematics, extremely creative, a poet at heart. She knew what the root of his problem was, but to address it openly, she was certain, would worsen the situation. Telling her husband that he had unwittingly inhibited Arthur's individuality by trying to make him into his own image and likeness would have set off a storm that would have damaged their relationship. So Valeria encouraged Arthur to leave the house, to develop his own course in life, so that he would realize his potential and find happiness; staying home would kill his spirit.

Robert, her youngest son, was having difficulty carrying out his responsibilities at home and at prep school. This worried Valeria, because it could stunt the development of his character. He was a witty, happy-go-lucky young man, who moved throughout life care-free, always seeking a 'fun time.' Handsome, he attracted young ladies, wore expensive clothes and was popular at parties given by his high-society friends. Pursuing the spiritual themes of life was boring to Robert. But his mother never stopped trying to lift her son's sights beyond the sensual. At times she would crack through his earthy armour, and find a little boy crying out for spiritual nourishment. The fact that he would from time to time reveal his spiritual side was enough encouragement for her to believe that one day he would discover reality.

For a while she thought that day had come, when she received Curtis' first letter from Haifa. It was the afternoon of November 26. After reading it, she entered the kitchen where Robert was eating lunch and shared the letter with him. She put her arm around Robert and both of them wept.

'It didn't sound like Curt,' he said. 'I think I'd like to go to the Bahá'í meetings again.'

Curtis' letter was long: five single-spaced typewritten pages, covering the major events from the day he landed in Haifa to October 31, the day he mailed it. She read it many times, for it helped to transport her to the Master's presence and to her dear son's side. The letter sparked her active imagination, living through Curtis' experiences, trying to inhale the spiritual fragrances that he breathed every day of his stay in the Holy Land. Going on pilgrimage, through her mind's eye, revived a deep yearning, which she had buried as impossible to realize. The fact that Curtis stated that Dr Ḥakím and the women at the World Center had urged her to come to the Holy Land in the spring helped her to decide to make the pilgrimage – and she would try to take Arthur and Robert along. Perhaps meeting 'Abdu'l-Bahá, she thought, would help them gain spiritual perspective and focus and put their lives in order. Her husband's coolness toward the Faith wasn't going to deter her from doing what she wanted more than anything else in the world. She wouldn't ask Frank to pay for the trip, because he wasn't a Bahá'í, but she would get the money somehow. Perhaps she might be able to secure an advance on her novel, or obtain a loan from a trusted friend.

The same day she received Curtis' letter, she sat down to write to the Master:

Dearly Beloved Master,
    'Abdu'l-Bahá!
Is it Thy will that I should visit Thee at Haifa, in time to return with my son Curtis?

There appears no outer possibility of this visit, but Thou knowest that through Thine inspiration and by the power of Thine assistance, this unworthy servant has written a book, *Immortal Cup*, and a play, *The Fountain*, and it may be that through these the way will open, should it be Thy will.

If it should be that Thou will allow me to go to Thee, may I bring one or both of my sons?

Mrs Latimer writes, urging me to make the journey with them in early spring.

The deepest desire of my heart is to see Thee and to serve Thee. I praise Thee for Thy Great Bounty to my son Curtis, and for the inestimable gifts passing all words to myself.

                              I am, with deep love,
                              Valeria DeMude Kelsey

Valeria was determined to go; but she didn't want to stir up disunity in the home. Telling Frank would be a sensitive undertaking; it would have to wait a week or two, because of the furor he had set off the previous day.

When Frank had walked into the house around noon on Thanksgiving Day and discovered his wife feeding two unemployed men lunch in the kitchen, he lost control and berated her for bringing 'bums into the house' – and threatened to leave the family if she continued to do such foolish things.

Frank's outbursts, his display of hard-heartedness and prejudice made her ill, often forcing her to bed for days. But Curtis' letter the next day chased away the pain of grief; now she could look forward to the possibility of seeing the Master. Only being with 'Abdu'l-Bahá would be a better medicine.

Chapter 8

'Get up! Get up! The Master! The Master!' someone cried, while pounding on the door of Curtis' room. Alarmed, the three young men inside awoke, jumped out of bed and groped in the dark for their clothes. It was about 1:00 A.M., November 28, and cool. But the weather didn't bother them, as they dashed to 'Abdu'l-Bahá's house, Curtis still tucking his shirt into his trousers.

As Curtis entered the house, people were weeping, some hysterically. He had to practically push his way through the crowd of people, mostly Persians, groaning and moaning, some wailing uncontrollably. When he reached the Master's room, Dr Florian Krug was standing beside the bed where 'Abdu'l-Bahá lay. The physician, who had arrived in Haifa with his wife two weeks earlier, turned to Curtis and said, 'The Master has just ascended.'

Dr Krug, a prominent New York doctor, who bitterly opposed the Faith when his wife embraced it, and then became a Bahá'í when he met 'Abdu'l-Bahá in America, closed the lids of the Master's eyes.

Curtis had never witnessed such deeply felt despair. For some reason, he couldn't show any emotion. That wasn't like him for he wasn't hard-hearted. Perhaps he wasn't faithful, he thought, and forced himself to cry; but he stopped when an inner voice commanded, 'No, not that; now is the time to observe.'

Curtis stood silently for a few moments, gazing at that mighty figure, on the bed, that had cast light into his life and helped him to understand and experience joy. It always felt good to be with Him, so good. He would have done anything for 'Abdu'l-Bahá. Curtis was too close to his Holy Land experiences to appreciate what the Master had taught him, breathed into him. But through the years it became evident little by little.

There was pandemonium in the main central room. Rúḥí Afnán, the Master's grandson, was sobbing, beating his head with his fists, and blaming the death of the Master on the American believers' disobedience. Of course, Curtis knew that wasn't true. Some people were crying out, as if asking God, 'Why does this have to happen? What will become of the Cause now that the Master is gone?'

The one who could answer those questions was across the room. The Greatest Holy Leaf calmly went about comforting the grief-stricken, absorbing their pain. As Curtis watched her move from person to person, stroking a shoulder, clasping a stretched-out hand, he noticed that she exhibited the kind of strength that 'Abdu'l-Bahá radiated. Some sensed that and clung to her. Her control, her poise, her unrestrained flow of compassion assured him that the Faith would not falter. She was, at that moment, the head of the Faith that her dear brother had led so successfully for twenty-nine years, giving His all. She was a tower of strength that all would rally around for support.

As he watched the Greatest Holy Leaf, her eyes caught his and she walked over to him. Since he was not crying, he wondered why she was coming toward him.

'Kelsey,' she said, 'will you take Fujita and Khusraw to 'Akká to tell the friends there of the Master's passing and then come right back?'

It was about two-thirty in the morning when they piled into the Master's Ford, with Curtis in the driver's seat, Fujita beside him and Khusraw in the back. There was no longer any chill in the air; in fact it was a balmy night; the same kind of night as when Curtis walked with the Master to Bahjí. The only sounds were the rhythmic beat of the surf washing over the beach and pulling back to the sea – and the near quiet crying of Fujita and Khusraw. Tears welled up in Curtis' eyes as he thought of 'Abdu'l-Bahá, and his experiences with Him during the past two months and he began to cry openly when he thought of what a shock the Master's passing would be to the friends across the world. It was more than losing a close friend, or a member of your family. So many would feel that their link with God had been severed.

Though Curtis was weeping, he kept driving. He couldn't stop, for the Greatest Holy Leaf wanted the believers in 'Akká to know about the passing of the Master. Curtis began to pray for strength.

Soon all three stopped crying, because they were approaching a stream that they had to cross in order to reach their destination. The car stopped, and Khusraw waded into the water, searching for a sand bar. Without one it would be impossible to drive across the stream, which fed into the Bay of Haifa. In a matter of minutes, K͟husraw found what he was looking for; and Curtis followed him, making it safely to shore. Soon they encountered another stream and conquered it in the same way.

Sharing the sad news with the friends, especially after waking them, was difficult. All of them expressed disbelief; some stared at the three young men as if what they had heard was part of a dream. Curtis' immediate instinct was to stay with the friends, to try to comfort them, but they had to be back as soon as possible. After urging the 'Akká friends to come to Haifa to attend the funeral, Curtis, Fujita and K͟husraw rushed back to Haifa to see what they could do next for the Greatest Holy Leaf.

They were cruising at about thirty miles per hour. At that pace they would be back in plenty of time to help with early morning chores at 'Abdu'l-Bahá's house. Getting over the first stream proved no problem, because they followed the tracks they had made going to 'Akká. Negotiating the second one appeared as easy – the tracks were still visible. But the sand bar wasn't where it was before; it had shifted and the car began to sink. All three scrambled out of the Ford, with Curtis yelling, 'Do what I do!'

Curtis, with water up to his hips, was lifting one of the front wheels, trying to keep it from touching the mucky stream floor. Fujita and K͟husraw were beside him, having difficulty with their footing. The water was up to Fujita's neck and K͟husraw's shoulders; and when they tried to lift the wheel, their legs gave way and they ended up floating and clinging to the running board. That wasn't going to be much help, Curtis thought. He couldn't allow the car to settle into the mud, yet he couldn't continue to bear most of the weight of the vehicle.

Remembering that before approaching the stream, about two miles away, he had noticed several husky Arab fishermen casting nets into the sea, Curtis asked <u>Kh</u>usraw to fetch them. While <u>Kh</u>usraw was gone, Curtis and Fujita moved from wheel to wheel ... trying to keep them from becoming captives of the mud. But keeping the car afloat wasn't their only worry. They felt they were needed back in Haifa because the Greatest Holy Leaf had said they should return immediately. Being stuck in a stream about nine miles from Haifa on the day of the Master's passing rankled Curtis.

In about thirty minutes Curtis noticed the fishermen coming, with <u>Kh</u>usraw leading the way; all of them talking loudly in Arabic and gesturing freely. They ran into the water, joining the weary Curtis and Fujita. With great ease, they lifted the car from the water and onto the shore pointing toward Haifa. After drying the carburetor, the three young Bahá'ís resumed their trip back to Haifa.

Even in death the Master was the cause of unity, advancing the principle of the oneness of humankind. People from all quarters of Haifa, poor and rich, marched side by side to 'Abdu'l-Bahá's house, where the casket rested. Others had come long distances to attend the Master's funeral. The High Commissioner of Palestine, Sir Herbert Samuel, the Governor of Phoenicia, the Governor of Jerusalem, Druze leaders from the Lebanon Mountains, Turks, Kurds, Arabs, Greeks, Egyptians, Germans, Swiss, Americans, Persians and British were a part of the spontaneous outpouring of respect for 'Abdu'l-Bahá that turned into a procession of about ten thousand. It was as if the Master were standing on the mountain top, arms outstretched, drawing the multitudes together as one family. Even the religious leaders, Anglican,

Roman Catholic and Greek Orthodox priests, along with the chiefs of the Muslim community and Jewish leaders, marched together united in their love and admiration for one they knew was brought to Palestine as a despised prisoner and who rose out of the bondage of injustice through His deep love and unqualified service to all. They knew how often His life was threatened; how small-minded men plotted to seize the Bahá'í properties, which he guarded like a lion; and in the crowd were those who at one time were infected by the poisonous rumours circulated by the enemies of the Faith and Covenant-breakers, but who grew to love the Master after meeting Him.

Everyone knew that 'Abdu'l-Bahá had helped to keep the people of Haifa and 'Akká from starving during World War One. 'Abdu'l-Bahá had often spent hours on His feet giving sacks of wheat, which he had grown Himself, to the poor of Haifa and 'Akká. There was no way they could repay Him for what He had done for them. No wonder merchants closed their shops, teachers shut down their school, and governmental officials left their desks to be at 'Abdu'l-Bahá's funeral. No one there could remember the likes of the human outpouring of appreciation and love that was afforded 'Abdu'l-Bahá. It was unprecedented.

The people marched slowly up Mount Carmel, passing the coffin containing the remains of the Master, from out-stretched hands to out-stretched hands. People vied with each other for the privilege of carrying the casket for only a moment. And they weren't Bahá'ís. For two hours they marched, as many wailed, 'O God! My God! Our Father has left us, our Father has left us!' Halfway to the Shrine of the Báb, a troop of Boy Scouts placed a wreath on the coffin.

For Curtis it was a time to observe, as that inner voice had commanded the night the Master passed away. And he was recording the historic event with the camera his mother had given him the day he left home for Haifa. He ran alongside of the procession, ran ahead, climbed steep cliffs to get pictures from all angles. It turned out that the photographs he took of the Master's funeral were among the best taken, and were later used in books.

When the procession finally reached the garden at the Shrine of the Báb, the casket, draped with a simple paisley shawl, was tenderly placed upon a plain table covered with a white linen cloth.

People pressed closer to the coffin, in a last expression of love for their dear, departed friend. There were nine speakers, leaders of the Jewish, Christian and Muslim communities. So glowing were their eulogies that there was no need for a Bahá'í speaker. With fervor and passion, they hailed Him as the true friend of the poor and downtrodden, praised Him for His work in developing understanding between different religions and different races and called Him the leader of mankind. The crowd heard a saint being described and they knew it was an accurate description, for many had been the recipients of His love and care.

Curtis heard the speeches in Arabic and French, and though he couldn't understand what was being said, he could feel the love and reverence in the voices of the orators, and the grief and sense of loss in the crowd. But despite all of the acclaim showered on the Master, Curtis knew that few people on that sunny day on Mount Carmel understood what 'Abdu'l-Bahá represented to humanity and what He was truly working for. Curtis knew that the Master was more than a saint.

The casket was lifted carefully from the table and placed on the broad shoulders of the Shrine's caretaker, who stepped slowly into the vault in the room next to the one sheltering the remains of the Báb. Only one man could take the casket down, for there was no room for anyone else. After the funeral, this same caretaker, a powerful man, realized why the Master had asked him a puzzling question the day before He passed away: 'You are a strong man. Could you not carry me away to a place where I could rest? I'm tired of this world.'

Chapter 9

For Curtis it was difficult to believe that the Master had gone. So powerful a personality had dominated everything on Mount Carmel through His love. Though He wasn't about anymore, walking down the mountain to feed a hungry child, to gently guide a dying woman into the next kingdom, or nurse a sick man, the spirit of the World Center and environs was unchanged. For nearly thirty years His continual reflection of Bahá'u'lláh's Revelation had created a new atmosphere; and it wasn't going to evaporate with His passing. It would remain forever, only to be enriched by Shoghi Effendi's spirit.

The Greatest Holy Leaf had quietly but firmly taken charge; and through her efforts she kept alive the rhythm that her brother had established at the World Center. The majority of the believers didn't sit around wallowing in grief. Work had to be done. Because the Cause of God is dynamic, its healing Message had to be shared with every soul on the planet; its institutions had to be established and strengthened; plans charted by the Master had to be fulfilled; the believers had to be nurtured and encouraged; and there was the divine charge to unite the human family. There was no time for sentimentality. And Curtis sensed that the Master would have it no other way, that the believers must press forward to construct what Bahá'u'lláh had envisioned. To strive to do as 'Abdu'l-Bahá had done, Curtis felt, would be the most fitting way to pay tribute to Him.

Curtis did that. He and Ḥusayn quickened their pace. In about two months, they felt, 'Abdu'l-Bahá's dream of illuminating both Shrines would materialize. Curtis was sure of that. He seemed to have more energy, a deeper belief that the lighting project would be completed the way the Master wanted it to be. Nothing, he felt, save God's intervention, could prevent that from happening. He worked like a man creating a gift for his Beloved.

Though Curtis was inspired, and he owed a lot to the Greatest Holy Leaf for inspiring him, there were some believers, especially some of the older ones, who seemed semi-paralyzed by the Master's passing. They missed Him, and openly expressed worry about the future of the Faith. Was there anyone with the vision and brilliance of the Master who could take charge, they wondered? It was comforting to know that 'Abdu'l-Bahá had left a Will and Testament. Did He name a successor, some asked aloud? Everyone knew that the Will and Testament was addressed to Shoghi Effendi Rabbani, a grandson of the Master, who was studying at Oxford University; but some of the older believers felt that a twenty-four-year-old lad didn't have the experience or wisdom to lead the Faith.

About thirty days after the Master's passing, Shoghi Effendi arrived in Haifa, apparently recovered from the shock of his beloved grandfather's death. In England the sad news had incapacitated him, forcing him to bed for several days.

But in Haifa, Curtis remembered Shoghi Effendi as being fit. He and several other young believers spoke with him at length the day before the Will was read. The young Oxford student, who was preparing to be a writer and the Master's translator, possessed a special bearing, radiating dignity and showering love on all who came into his presence. Curtis was also struck by Shoghi Effendi's humility; it was something rarely exhibited by young people in his day. There was also an air of innocence about Shoghi Effendi that no doubt sprang from his purity of heart. That, more than anything else, impressed Curtis.

The next day a large gathering squeezed into the central room of the Master's house to hear the Will and Testament read. The text was clear: Shoghi Effendi had been appointed Guardian of the Faith, the sole interpreter of the Revelation on Earth; the Head of a world faith that had a divine mandate to lift humanity from the quicksand of materialism to verdant heights of spirituality, to help people everywhere see and integrate into their beings the reality of the oneness of humankind, to establish a world society engineered from plans conceived by God and shared with us through Bahá'u'lláh – a stupendous undertaking. No wonder Shoghi Effendi, that sensitive soul, was shaken, forced to bed for several days, unable to eat. The weight of the world had been passed onto his shoulders, the one who wanted only to serve the Master, to be His translator, who never aspired to any leadership role in the Faith, nor ever thought of such a possibility. To this humble, radiant youth was handed the mantle of directorship of God's Cause.

Many of the people who heard the Master's Will and

Testament read remained in 'Abdu'l-Bahá's house most of
the day carefully going over every sentence, trying to gain
some insight as to where the Faith was headed. When the
meeting adjourned, Curtis remembered seeing a number of
men walking out weeping. They were shedding tears of joy,
for the Master, in appointing Shoghi Effendi as Guardian,
had protected the future of the Cause of God.

In a few days, Shoghi Effendi was back among the friends,
recovered from the initial shock of being appointed
Guardian, but obviously a young man with a lot more on his
mind than when he arrived in Haifa.

One evening, Shoghi Effendi noticed Curtis in the street
and asked that he join him in a walk on Mount Carmel
Avenue, which led to the Shrine of the Báb. Curtis knew that
it wasn't going to be an ordinary walk, for the young man
walking beside him was now more than a faithful grandson of
'Abdu'l-Bahá: he was the Guardian. Maybe, he wondered,
the Guardian would give him a special assignment. Curtis
didn't know what to expect.

As they walked up the road, children were dancing in the
shadows cast over the street by the floodlight perched at the
base of the Shrine. Electricity was new to the people of Haifa.
No one had it in their homes. Seeing shadows in the evening
was odd; and the children turned them into a form of
recreation. Of course, none of them knew that the man who
made the shadows possible was in their midst and beside him
was the 'sign of God' on earth.

As they walked up the mountain, Shoghi Effendi turned to
Curtis and thanked him for the wonderful work he had done
in installing the three electrical plants and pointed out how
much the Master appreciated his efforts.

The praise made Curtis uncomfortable; and he blushed, saying, 'Well, Shoghi Effendi, I was very happy doing the work for the Master, and I want no credit.'

The Guardian stopped walking and looked into Curtis' eyes and said firmly, 'Nevertheless appreciation goes with your service.'

When Curtis tried to make light of his work, the Guardian grew firmer, making an issue of the importance of sincerely thanking a person for the services he renders. For Curtis it was an important lesson. After that experience, he always made sure to share his gratitude with the person who did work for him, however small the task.

Several days later Shoghi Effendi was gone, off to Germany, and then Switzerland, for an unspecified amount of time, where he would be alone, fortifying himself for something he had never planned on doing. Someone other than himself had committed him to a life-long challenge that he had not consciously prepared for; it would be a time of sorting out his thoughts, in discovering, with God's help, how to direct an infant World Faith toward maturity.

With Shoghi Effendi in Europe, the Greatest Holy Leaf took charge. Curtis and Ḥusayn had virtually completed the lighting project. Only a few superficial things were left to fix. There was nothing more to do. The Guardian hadn't given Curtis any assignments. The thought of returning to America began to surface. Strange, but Curtis didn't think of that powerful nation across the Atlantic as home. In his heart, Curtis knew that his real home was in Haifa and Bahjí. He remembered how his mother, who had never been to the Holy Land, would comment on how her real home was where the Master dwelt.

It was sad that his mother had never made her pilgrimage. She came so close. He knew what courage it took for her to decide to go to Haifa. The letter Valeria Kelsey wrote to the Master, asking for permission to go on pilgrimage, was sent to him to pass on to 'Abdu'l-Bahá. But it arrived a month after 'Abdu'l-Bahá's passing. Curtis had read the letter that had been written shortly before 'Abdu'l-Bahá's death. By reading it, Curtis gained an understanding of his mother's yearning to meet 'Abdu'l-Bahá. There was little else in the world that was more important than that personal wish. It turned out that Valeria Kelsey's dream was realized. That became apparent in a letter to Curtis from his mother, which he received late in February: 'A few nights ago I had a wonderful dream of 'Abdu'l-Bahá, in which I saw Him. It seemed that I saw a great crowd of people, and between me and them was an open gate. Suddenly, as I watched this crowd, 'Abdu'l-Bahá came out from the center of it, and came towards me, His white robes sweeping away behind him with the swiftness of His movement. He was smiling, and I had a moment of panic, realizing that He was going to put His arms about me, and that I was foolishly tall! Then, before I knew it, He swept through the gate and folded me in His arms. I could not breathe; it seemed that I would suffocate, and that was the end of the dream ... You will have to be the interpreter. I certainly cannot tell what it means, but it made me happy to have seen Him, if only in a dream.'

What 'Abdu'l-Bahá had envisioned materialized: the lights at the Shrines of Bahá'u'lláh and the Báb were turned on at the same time, and because electricity wasn't widespread in the Haifa–'Akká area, the two brilliant lights excited the populace. They had never seen anything like that before.

Though twelve miles apart, the light emanating from each place seemed to be reaching out to the other. Everyone at the World Center was thrilled to see what the Master longed for come about. There were those, including Curtis, who wished that 'Abdu'l-Bahá had lived to watch the lights go on at both shrines simultaneously. They had witnessed Him endure so much hardship, and for Him not to be present to experience such a momentous triumph seemed unfair. Years later, Curtis realized that in reality it didn't matter that the Master wasn't around for the lighting ceremony, because the day he put the project in motion He must have experienced the victory; He knew that it would be completed as He specified. It would only be a matter of human time and effort before what He saw with His mind's eye would come into being.

Much more happened to Curtis while in Palestine than gaining the satisfaction of developing something that was so dear to 'Abdu'l-Bahá. Now that he was ready to go back to America, Curtis sensed that he was not the same person who had arrived in Haifa on that hot, sun-blazing day in September. He couldn't articulate what changes had taken place. It took being back in New York, working and dealing with a world that found it more and more fashionable to avoid spiritual challenges, to realize what had been imbued in him by being exposed to the Master at such close range. The strength secured from his Holy Land experience seemed to well up in him whenever tested. Without that, Curtis knew, life would have been a burden. Reality was what he had experienced in Haifa, 'Akká and Bahjí. And he never forgot that, even when he slipped from the Bahá'í standard. What most people were exposed to day after day was a maelstrom of confusion, uncertainty, fear and flights of fantasy. And they accepted that as reality. Because Curtis knew differently, he felt compelled to help others feel what he felt and know what he knew. Not doing that would have been a great disservice to all those he encountered.

During the last days of his stay in Haifa, Curtis didn't concern himself with how he would return to New York, even though he only had enough money to reach Constantinople. Somehow the means would become available. If it didn't, he thought, he could always secure some employment in Turkey and earn enough money for a passage to America. But unbeknown to him others were aware of his economic situation. One day while packing for his trip home, Curtis was asked to come to the Master's house. When he arrived he was led to 'Abdu'l-Bahá's room where he found the Greatest Holy Leaf and three of the Master's daughters waiting for him. After greeting him warmly, they moved closer to him, actually encircling him. One of the daughters praised him for the work he had done. Remembering what he had learned from Shoghi Effendi, he accepted the expression of gratitude, but not without some effort. Overcoming ingrained habits isn't easy. But when that same daughter insisted that he take money for his trip home, Curtis said, 'No, all my affairs are in order.' He couldn't think of taking money from the Master's family. But the other daughters were adamant about the importance of his taking the money. He was equally adamant in refusing it. Finally, the Greatest Holy Leaf reached out and, taking hold of Curtis' hand, said, 'Kelsey, you need this money to pay for your return home,' and she placed the money in his hand.

'I will take it,' Curtis said, 'if you will let me return it after getting home.'

'No,' she responded firmly.

Curtis sensed that the Greatest Holy Leaf had issued a divine command reminiscent of the way 'Abdu'l-Bahá responded when firmness was called for. Curtis graciously accepted the money and thanked them for it. He left the room, wondering how they knew what his financial condition was, when he hadn't told a soul about it.

Chapter 10

During the trip back to the United States there was plenty of time to reflect on what he had seen and felt while in the Holy Land. Curtis knew that those were precious times, and he wondered if he would ever return. As he drew closer to New York, he sensed that one day he would be walking on Mount Carmel again. With that feeling locked in some deep chamber of his heart, he returned to New York eager to plunge into the world he had left behind the day he set sail for Haifa.

He grew anxious when he thought of seeing his family, being with his friends and sharing his Holy Land experiences with them. The condition of the Faith in New York and elsewhere in the country concerned him. How were the friends taking the passing of the Master? Were they able to understand the purpose of the Guardianship? For Curtis the transition from 'Abdu'l-Bahá to Shoghi Effendi was easy to accept. But he had heard in Haifa of some misunderstanding in the United States concerning the appointment of Shoghi Effendi as Guardian. Perhaps, he felt, he could help put some troubled minds to rest. He had felt the power of the Cause up close. There was no doubt in his mind that God was guiding Shoghi Effendi. He sensed it the day he took that long walk with him.

Though 6,000 miles away from Haifa, and unable to see and feel what Curtis experienced, Valeria Kelsey shared her son's steadfastness and enthusiasm for the Guardian. A few days before Curtis' return, a letter from the Greatest Holy Leaf set her spirit sailing:

My dear sister in this blessed Cause,

... Mr Curtis Kelsey is leaving after a sojourn of hard work recompensated by the blessings of our Lord from on high and the affection of each and everyone who happened to come in contact with him; we thought that at this hour, when he is to leave us with perhaps a faint ray of hope to see us again, we would write a few words and express our idea of the sincerity and absolute devotion with which your son accomplished his allotted task and we would be in turn congratulating you for this achievement and assuring you that [each and] every time that we see those bright lights shining from those blessed Tombs we cannot but remember that sincere and diligent work which was put into it and the sacrifice of Mr Wilhelm who supplied the necessary material.

We earnestly hope that this will be the first of the services by which Mr Kelsey is to prove his devotion to our dear Lord, and we are sure that His grace shall ever help him in his lifetime.

Our sincerest greetings to all of the Bahá'í friends there.

I remain, Your sister in His love,
Greatest Holy Leaf

Curtis' home-coming helped to defuse some of the tension in the Kelsey household. Everyone was eager to know about his experiences. Away for eight months in a place whose history is recorded in the Bible, Curtis was viewed as some sort of global adventurer. To his brothers he was more than a brother who had been away from home for a while. He was considered as someone who was spiritually special. They were proud of him. So was his father; but for a different reason. Frank Kelsey admired Curtis' resourcefulness, independence of mind and inner strength. The fact that he went halfway around the world to a strange place, overcoming cultural differences and living through hardships, and designed and completed a major construction project – that impressed Curtis' father. It also reinforced his need to draw closer to his favorite son. Curtis, he felt, was more like him than any of the other children. To Arthur his father's preference for Curtis was obvious. All he ever felt from him was hostility and contempt. Though he tried to heed his mother's advice about going into the world on his own, he kept returning home, most likely seeking the affection that his father always denied him. Curtis was aware of the antipathy between his father and oldest brother and could do nothing to end their feud. He knew how much that kind of family friction hurt his mother. She looked older and behind her warm smile he sensed torment. Playing peacemaker, in a household where her husband viewed peace as everyone bowing to his demands without question, was difficult for Valeria, who was so appalled by injustice that whenever she encountered it she would become sick. While Curtis was gone, she was often ill. He knew that from the tone of her letters. To lift her spirit, he spent hours alone with his mother, relating his experiences with 'Abdu'l-Bahá and answering her many questions. Curtis tried hard to take his mother on pilgrimage through his memory and feelings. From the way she responded, he seemed to have fulfilled his wish.

In 1922 the development of the Bahá'í community was as yet immature. Even the most erudite had difficulty understanding many aspects of it. With many of the believers, the passing of the Master was almost too much to bear. They had never known anyone at the helm of the Faith except 'Abdu'l-Bahá. His loss set off a campaign of faultfinding in the New York Community. It seemed that some of the grieving ones needed a scapegoat. Rumours were circulated against Roy Wilhelm and Mountfort Mills – both members of the New York City Local Spiritual Assembly, and these stories reached Roy shortly after Curtis' return, hurting him deeply. His helplessness to stop the rumours frustrated him. Curtis was aware of Roy's plight, had even heard people making these accusations. Curtis tried to assure Roy that in Haifa no one believed the stories, that they were fabricated by misguided or jealous people. Though appreciated, Curtis' attempt to soothe Roy's spirit failed; but soon the Master answered Roy's pleas for help from the Abhá Kingdom in the form of a dream. In the dream, Roy was sitting beside the Master in His high buckboard wagon, with 'Abdu'l Bahá handling the reins. It was so real that Roy could feel the heat of the Master's body. While driving, 'Abdu'l-Bahá turned, facing Roy squarely, smiling and saying, 'But you would still have Me.' When Roy awoke, that gnawing feeling of having been abused, having been treated unjustly had vanished. He felt happy again, as the Master had always asked the friends to be, and he was back serving the Guardian as he had served 'Abdu'l-Bahá.

Having lived and worked in the Holy Land for eight months, and having attended the Master's funeral, Curtis was treated like a celebrity by many of the believers. He was asked to speak at Bahá'í gatherings and had lots of dinner invitations from people who were starved for information about 'Abdu'l-Bahá. Curtis' lighting work at Haifa and Bahjí wasn't overlooked. Many people thanked him and congratulated him on his efforts.

The adulation directed at Curtis set off a mixed reaction in him. Part of him enjoyed the attention he was receiving; but another part couldn't understand why people were making such a fuss over him. All he did, he felt, was go over to Haifa and Bahjí to install some lighting plants. He wasn't used to such praise, and he was awkward dealing with it.

Returning to work with his father helped Curtis move out of the light of prominence in the New York area. He was back in the field, supervising the construction of large wood-stave pipelines all over New England. Business was good and Curtis showed considerable ability as an engineer even though he lacked formal schooling. He learned quickly, especially by doing, and by observing professionals operate. Curtis became the apple of his father's eye. Frank Kelsey marveled over his son's ability to adjust to new situations. Curtis swung back to work as if he had not been gone at all. His ability to solve mechanical problems quickly and efficiently impressed his father. The fact that Frank Kelsey drew closer to his son made him less irritable.

Though seriously involved in his work, Curtis was still committed to the Faith. It was the first love of his life. How could it be otherwise after having gazed into the eyes of 'Abdu'l-Bahá? But his love for the Faith was different than it had been previous to his journey to Haifa. At that point he felt himself on a steed galloping toward enchantment – no other direction mattered. But back from the Holy Land, he was wiser. He realized that being a Bahá'í meant more than being enamored of the Teachings; it meant manifesting the Teachings in everyday life, serving others as the Master did – living a balanced life. He realized also that he had the responsibility of unifying his family. More attention to his father, he felt, was the key.

Both his mother and father approved of Una Martin, Curtis' girlfriend whom he had met prior to his army experience. She was a well-mannered, attractive young lady who was spiritually inclined. Most people who knew the two thought they would marry one day. But Curtis wasn't thinking about marriage. The Faith and developing his professional career occupied most of his thoughts. He enjoyed Una's company but didn't miss her when she wasn't around. He knew he would never marry her.

But Una unwittingly helped to shape an important part of Curtis' future by introducing him to the woman he would eventually marry. One day, prior to his trip to Haifa, while walking down a New York City street, Una asked Curtis to stop for a moment; a friend of hers was approaching. It was Harriet Morgan, a pretty young lady who had come from Niagara Falls to study piano in New York. Una had met her at Bahá'í firesides, even at Valeria Kelsey's firesides. After reading the *Hidden Words*, which Una had loaned her, Harriet knew Bahá'u'lláh was the return of Christ.

Harriet had heard of Curtis. For that matter, most young Bahá'í ladies were aware of him, considering him a very eligible bachelor. Now he was facing her, tall, handsome and reserved. As she stood there, something happened to her which she couldn't control – her heart started beating faster as she was introduced to him. Whatever Harriet said to Una had nothing, absolutely nothing to do with how she felt. Harriet knew the moment she looked into Curtis' face that she was attracted to him. But Curtis didn't flash even the most subtle sign of being moved.

Harriet encountered Curtis again at different Bahá'í gatherings, including the Kelseys' place. She created opportunities to speak to him, but couldn't detect any spark.

When Curtis returned from the Holy Land, he and Harriet were twenty-seven. Though Harriet looked younger than that, she was conscious of her age. Most healthy women were married at her age. She feared growing old alone, as a frustrated spinster. In those days, if a woman wasn't married by the age of twenty-two, friends and relatives suspected that something was wrong with her. Like most people, Harriet detested being a topic of gossip; and she sensed people were talking about her.

Getting married wasn't as easy for Harriet as for most other young women. She had to support her mother as well as herself. Her six sisters and brothers – all older than her – were married and couldn't afford the added expense. Harriet held several jobs at once, playing the organ at a church and the piano in a movie house, which was a challenge. She had to make up music spontaneously to fit the mood and tone of the action on the silent screen. Attending firesides, being coached in piano and practicing also took up a lot of time and energy. Much to Harriet's regret, her mother proved to be an obstacle to her marrying. Almost every suitor who came to the house was cornered by her mother and discouraged from coming back by her statement, 'Harriet is not interested in marriage, for she is wedded to her music.'

Valeria Kelsey became a close friend of Harriet, getting to know her before Curtis was introduced to her. Valeria was particularly fond of Harriet's plucky spirit and humility. Both often had long heart-to-heart talks. Though Harriet never mentioned how she felt about Curtis, Valeria sensed that Harriet loved him, and that the two were suited for each other. But Valeria never interfered in Curtis' personal life, although at times she was tempted to try to open her son's eyes so he could see Harriet's true value. In fact, a few times Curtis' blindness concerning the young lady from Niagara Falls so infuriated Valeria that she wanted to 'knock some sense' into him.

For years Harriet hoped Curtis would be drawn to her, but she received no encouragement from him. At thirty she accepted a marriage proposal from Jack Bristol, a sensitive artist from Norway, Maine, about 300 miles from New York City. Though married, Harriet couldn't rub out of her consciousness that young man who had been 'Abdu'l Bahá's electrician. Despite that special feeling for Curtis, Harriet was a faithful wife to Jack Bristol. In about a year she gave birth to a girl; but shortly after that happy event, Jack grew emotionally disturbed. When his condition worsened, Harriet was granted a divorce, with complete custody of her one-year-old daughter, Mary Louise. It was the lowest point of her life. Where to go? What to do next? She prayed fervently for protection, because she couldn't endure another setback. If it came, she knew she would break down, and her baby would be motherless. New York City – she was attracted to New York. But it wasn't the excitement of the city that lured her. It was, rather, the hope of encountering Curtis, maybe at a fireside, a Feast, even in the street. Harriet packed her belongings and with her daughter headed back to New York.

When Harriet returned to New York, Curtis wasn't in any condition to marry. The passing of his mother had not only created a great emotional gap in his life, but he had also vowed not to marry until he was certain his father was more emotionally secure.

Frank Kelsey was deeply shaken by his wife's passing. Though he had been frustrated by things she believed in and did, he truly loved Valeria. He knew she cared for him. The anger that he often directed at her was really aimed at smashing the invisible barrier that stood between them. To him the barrier was the Faith, something he knew meant more to her than anything else in her life. Jealousy and pride kept him from investigating the Faith. Yet there was a part of him that knew that had he embraced Bahá'u'lláh their marriage would have been stronger. But something within him, something he didn't like, prevented him from taking the step that would have thrown his wife into his arms. He hated himself for being so bull-headed. In a way, he sensed that after her accident she didn't have the will to live. Valeria had fallen down a flight of stairs. Badly bruised, she was confined to her bed. Complications developed: she was seized by a series of convulsions. The fever mystified the family doctor, because she wasn't combating a disease. Watching his wife waste away infuriated her husband, because he was a fighter. No one should die from tumbling down stairs, he felt. If only he could infuse his will into her. But Frank Kelsey couldn't appreciate his wife's view of the 'after life.' He was a survivor, who would fight for every second of life. Immortality of the soul was a concept he had difficulty comprehending. But his wife didn't harbor a shred of doubt about life continuing beyond the earthly experience.

At fifty-four she was tired of the tension and conflict in her life. The feud between Frank and their eldest son seemed beyond correction. That kind of futility caused a constant heartache. If only Frank could forgive Arthur for running away from the Marines during the war. He detested quitters. He couldn't believe a son of his could commit such a cowardly and irresponsible act, and become a fugitive of military law. But Frank couldn't understand what his wife saw and felt: Arthur was too sensitive to endure the bestiality of Marine boot camp. She was convinced that Frank would never understand.

It seemed also that the more involved she became in the Revelation, the more distant Frank became toward her. How she prayed for him! But the older he grew the more irritable and hard hearted he became and his outbursts of temper increased and intensified. She couldn't abide his rage. Every time that happened it was like being stabbed with a dagger.

Being a woman in 1924 was frustrating. There was so much she wanted to do but couldn't because custom had chained her to her 'place.' Only in Bahá'í circles did she feel freer; women were elected to the Local Spiritual Assembly and appointed to important committees. But even there most of the men didn't fully understand and appreciate Bahá'u'lláh's principle of the equality of the sexes – and she ran into barriers. There was a part of her that wanted to cry out publicly against the injustices perpetuated against womanhood. She had the stuff that makes a Joan of Arc. Her devotion to the Faith, however, kept her from organizing and leading demonstrations against the establishment. Waging campaigns against female discrimination would have undermined whatever family unity she had labored to develop. She knew Frank would leave her if she became a crusader for women's rights. She believed that through Bahá'u'lláh, equality of the sexes would be achieved by the process of unifying the human family.

Because she was so seriously ill, she became increasingly resigned to passing into the 'next life.' She had no fear of leaving this world. In fact, the prospect of meeting her daughter Katherine, her son Allen and her father in the next world appealed to her. But more so did the possibility of being greeted by 'Abdu'l-Bahá.

A few days before she passed away Valeria seemed happy, like a prospective voyager waiting to embark on a trip to a place where she longed to be. That day she received a bunch of daffodils and sweet peas, and was moved to write: 'Daffodils – golden filaments of remembrance from out the flying hours, and sweet peas, a promise of summer soon to come, lovely heralds of beauty. When I see them, it is to reflect upon the limitless power and love of God, who creates out of his own joy the unending round of color in this transient world: sun, seasons, hours, flashing and flaming in unquenchable joy beyond our comprehension.

'And your prayers for me, dear friends, perhaps it may be that they come to fruition in the Garden of God, where He walks at eventide. What? God walks in gardens? – I am very sure He walks in mine.'

Chapter 11

Two years after the passing of his wife, Frank Kelsey remarried. Curtis wasn't opposed to his father's remarrying, but he had serious reservations about the woman whom he chose as his second wife. Marjorie Milleron, Curtis suspected, was more interested in his father's money than in him. He felt strongly about this and shared his feelings with his father, which wasn't easy, because he didn't want to pry into his father's personal life. Only after he was convinced of his motive, which was to save his father from an unhappy entanglement, did he approach him. But Curtis' appeal went unheeded.

Though he disapproved of the marriage, it did have a liberating effect on him. He was now free to do as he pleased, no longer needing to nurture his father. His father could fend for himself. If he wanted to, Curtis could start his own family; and he started thinking about that shortly after his father's wedding. For a thirty-two-year-old it was perfectly natural to think about marriage and the children that would result from it.

Because of his new attitude, he started noticing people who

had never intrigued him before, especially that pianist from Niagara Falls, who seemed to turn up at every fireside and Feast he attended. The fact that Harriet Morgan had been recently divorced didn't disturb him, something that was counter to his puritanical attitude toward women and marriage. Before his new outlook Curtis would have avoided a divorced woman, especially someone with a child. But for some strange reason, which he couldn't fathom at the time, he was attracted to Harriet, after nine years of encountering her at meetings. Only years later was he able to grasp some understanding as to his change of heart. It was his mother, in the Celestial Concourse, he was convinced, who did what she neglected to do while alive – and that was to open his eyes to the true value of Harriet, as well as knock some sense into him.

Realistically, Curtis wasn't ready for marriage when he and Harriet decided to marry. Not because he didn't love Harriet. There was no question about that. But he had never given it much serious thought. Work and the Faith took up most of his time. And there was his independent nature that could break out into rebelliousness if excessively pressurized. Fortunately, his deep commitment to Bahá'u'lláh had his nature under control. His lack of sensitivity about the needs of the opposite sex was another reason why he wasn't prepared for marriage, even at the age of thirty-three. His tendency toward being a loner was also a factor.

But Harriet, a wise woman, was aware of many of Curtis' foibles and unpreparedness for marriage. She knew he loved her and there was no question about her long-suffering feelings about him. What assured her that the marriage would not only last but strengthen over the years was their genuine dependency on Bahá'u'lláh in confronting life's challenges. And she proved to be right. That doesn't mean there weren't any problems and conflicts in their marriage, as well as heartache and anguish. They both experienced it, and because they learned from their tests, they grew closer as husband and wife.

Perhaps the first test occurred on their honeymoon, which is normally a very private affair. But evidently Curtis didn't think so, because he invited some of his closest friends – Roy Wilhelm, 'Al'áí Kalántar, Emily Moore and her mother, to join Harriet and him on their honeymoon, which turned out to be a camping trip in the White Mountains of New Hampshire.

Harriet could accept that kind of unorthodox behavior, because she knew that her new husband's motives were pure. Why not have those who are closest to you share in the joy of the marriage celebration? Curtis sincerely felt. Of course, their friends had their own tents.

Harriet survived the honeymoon without any deep misgivings or disappointments, even though her husband had broken a long-standing marriage custom. She knew it wouldn't be the last time Curtis would flaunt an accepted custom. She knew also that he wasn't the kind of person who would do something different for the sake of being different. Whatever he did, which most people would consider strange or unorthodox, was done because Curtis felt strongly that it was the right thing to do. In some respects he was an iconoclast. He had little tolerance for impractical and senseless practices. With that kind of attitude he showed considerable courage and confidence, which fired his drive to tackle any challenge that came his way. Actually, Harriet found that quality appealing, because by nature she was an iconoclast also, but a less audacious one. Curtis' assertiveness helped her to be more daring. So the honeymoon experience wasn't shocking; in fact, she not only eventually adapted and had a good time, but also discovered another reason for loving Curtis.

Though in love, married and employed in something he enjoyed doing, Curtis' primary concern was the Faith. He never hid that priority of interests from Harriet. In fact, she agreed that that was the way it should be; because she believed that by loving God first the love between husband and wife would grow greater. With that understanding, she could easily accept Curtis' desire to pioneer, to leave New York to help build a Bahá'í community elsewhere. Curtis' suggestion of moving to Teaneck, New Jersey was acceptable to Harriet; who was busy being a mother, not only to Mary Louise but to her infant son Allyn and to the new life within her womb.

Pioneering meant altering Curtis' employment pattern. In order to teach effectively, he felt, you had to work in the area where you lived. For that was a sensible means of attracting seekers. Leaving his father's firm wasn't as heart-wrenching as it could have been prior to his father's remarriage. With Marjorie becoming involved in the operation of the Continental Pipe Manufacturing Company, a communications chasm emerged between his father and himself. Curtis resented her influence on Mr Kelsey, because she had little knowledge of the business and no experience in it. Remaining full-time at the company, he felt, would only exacerbate the tense situation. So he left Continental, with the understanding that he would be available to do odd supervisory field jobs from time to time.

It didn't surprise Harriet that Curtis would tackle something he had never done before, because that was characteristic of him. She had her reservations about the practicality of Curtis' latest venture; but she had faith that 'it would all work out for the best.' Curtis opened an electrical shop, selling appliances and repairing any household item that ran on electricity. Starting a business in 1930 was poor timing. The nation was in its worst economic depression. But that didn't stop Curtis from forging ahead with his new adventure; nor did it restrain him from convincing his friend, a young American-educated Persian chemist, 'Al'áí Kalántar, to leave New York for a pioneering post in Teaneck, and to set up an oriental rug shop near his store. The trouble was that not many people were buying refrigerators and radios; and as for purchasing Persian rugs, that was as unlikely as flying to New York on a carpet. Businesses were collapsing at an unprecedented rate; unemployment was soaring. And two new entrepreneurs in Teaneck – Kelsey and Kalántar – stocked with heavy inventories, were struggling from being added to the list of business failures. Somehow, Curtis managed to scrape up enough money for groceries, mainly by fixing a few toasters, alarm clocks and radios, and doing odd jobs for his father. His shining appliances and luxury gadgets were virtually museum pieces except that they were in his store through the grace of credit. And that meant paying the manufacturer a monthly fee, which he couldn't always do. Prayer and quick thinking and quick talking were necessary in order to keep the collection people from removing his stock. But 'Al'áí wasn't as fortunate. In fact, Curtis recalled that whenever he stopped by the rug shop, he rarely noticed a customer inside.

He would invariably find 'Al'áí sitting on a pile of expensive imported rugs, with his legs crossed, looking like an oriental sage engrossed in the text resting on his lap. It was only a matter of months before the creditors took back the rugs, but 'Al'áí didn't leave his pioneering post; he found a job as a chemist in a local hospital. That cheered Curtis, for he wanted so to see a Local Spiritual Assembly spring up in the Teaneck area. No earthly force was going to draw him from where he was. While the bills mounted and the credit collectors hounded him, he pondered how he could earn a living in northern New Jersey should his inventory be seized. So intense was his desire to stay in Teaneck and teach the Faith effectively, he thought of ways of staying in the town. The best way to do that, he felt, was to purchase a house. But buy a house in the midst of a crippling depression, with barely enough money to provide three meager meals a day; and Harriet pregnant again with a fourth child? Any reasonable real estate counselor would have discouraged Curtis from even trying to consider buying property. But Curtis didn't seek professional advice. He listened to his intuition and persisted in finding a way to achieve his goal. Even to Harriet, Curtis' latest enterprise seemed beyond his long reach; but she knew that if it was God's will, then what seemed impossible would become possible. So she prayed that Curtis and her family would receive Divine assistance. When it came to prayer, incidentally, Harriet had enormous energy and stamina, something Curtis and her children grew to respect. Saying the Remover of Difficulties 1,000 times, when crisis engulfed the family, wasn't uncommon for Harriet. Knowing that his wife was beseeching help from the Celestial Concourse was comforting to Curtis. To him, that was more fundamental in life than anything else, even a low-interest mortgage.

While Curtis wondered how he was going to get the money for a house, he had found a place he wanted. It wasn't something that Harriet considered her dream-house, for it wasn't the typical American house. In fact, it looked foreign in a neighborhood of colonial and Cape Cod dwellings. Number 499 Grenville Avenue was a pink, one-floor, stucco Mediterranean-style bungalow, with exterior and interior arches, a flat red-tiled roof, and a façade that would fit naturally in Damascus or Jerusalem. With a corner lot, Curtis would be able to grow a vegetable garden, plant fruit trees, line the property with fragrant flowers, much like the gardens surrounding the Shrine of the Báb.

Though a test to her aesthetic taste, Harriet didn't discourage Curtis from trying to buy that house, because she knew the reason why he wanted it: the dwelling reminded him of Haifa, of those wondrous times on Mount Carmel, in Bahjí.

Curtis got the $6,000 he needed to buy the place from his father. Frank Kelsey knew that Curtis would never ask for the loan if he had any reservation about returning the money, even with interest. How to secure the money to pay off his creditors didn't plague Curtis; but it concerned him, because he had been brought up to believe that being a 'deadbeat' was as repugnant as being a liar. Curtis was a natural optimist. With time, a healthy body and a clear mind, he believed, he could tackle almost any problem. But it wasn't only optimism that allowed him to be adventurous. He took to heart 'Abdu'l-Bahá's exhortation, 'Be not idle, but active, and fear not.'

When Curtis and Harriet moved into their house, they had four children; the youngest, Carol, was three months. Mary Louise, who was six, was already her mother's helper, looking after Allyn, two-and-a-half, and June, one-and-a-half, when Harriet was busy washing, cooking, stoking the coal burner or practicing the piano. Though the family was happy leaving the cramped apartment for a seven-room house, on a large lot, they weren't moving into a palace. Repairs were needed, which Curtis confronted immediately. For years they were without a sofa in the living room, using wicker chairs instead, the kind of furniture you normally see in rustic summer cottages. But the lack of appropriate furniture didn't deter Curtis and Harriet from holding weekly firesides. In fact they never entertained any reservations about having Bahá'í meetings because of the house's simple and meager décor. The love and warmth that permeated that home made the interior of the house glow. Guests rarely remembered the primitive furnishings. It was the spirit that so impressed them that they would look forward to returning. Their closest neighbors, staunch Protestants, who were financially secure, and living in more substantial, richly furnished houses, were attracted to the Kelseys' odd-looking dwelling. Frank Fredericks, an arranger for the Paul Whiteman Orchestra and musical editor for Maestro Arturo Toscanini, and his wife Octavia were refreshed whenever they visited the drafty pink bungalow across the road from their large red-brick colonial home. They and their son Frank, Jr. eventually became Bahá'ís. William and Margaret Brooks, who lived in the neighborhood near the Kelseys, in an English Tudor house, embraced Bahá'u'lláh. So did their three children, Margaret (Peggy), Bill and Jim. It wasn't only the spirit in the house that attracted the Brooks and Fredericks families: Curtis and Harriet prayed for their spiritual awakening, loved them and served them, especially in times of greatest need.

Teaching so dominated their lives that they believed it was as natural a need as sleeping and eating. As long as the Kelsey children could remember there were weekly firesides in their home. Though every penny earned was carefully budgeted, Curtis always found funds to bake something for the firesides and serve tea and coffee. To them, skimping on fireside refreshments was like denying their children supper. Firesides not only became a normal event for the family, but word spread throughout the area about the attractiveness of the meetings being held in that strange looking pink place on Grenville Avenue. For Curtis, the fireside was the most important event, the happiest time of the week.

Because teaching was an essential part of Curtis' life, opportunities to share the message of Bahá'u'lláh with others arose at work, at times attracting people with the strangest backgrounds. Archie Tichenor, a dashing, fast talking appliance salesman, who believed anything could be sold, was a natural searcher of truth. In fact, his quest was so active that it irritated his wife Agnes. While married, Archie probed for the truth, going in many different, often opposite ideological directions. He joined and quit several Socialist groups, flirted with Communism, was a member of the Ku Klux Klan, an ardent believer in Masonry, an enthusiastic Republican. He investigated Buddhism, Hinduism, Christian Science, Roman Catholicism. He yearned for knowledge, for he felt only that would lead him to the object of his search. In Teaneck one day, Archie shared his views of life, and what he was seeking, with one of his customers. The man said there was an electrician in town who might have the answers to questions Archie posed. In fact, the man said, 'You two would have a lot in common.' Intrigued, Archie dashed to the struggling electrician and was impressed with the lanky, open-faced man behind the counter. Unlike most of the people he met during those early Depression days Curtis was genuinely happy. That impression set off an instantaneous attraction to Curtis. 'Either the guy is screwy,' Archie thought, 'or he knows something that I should know.' When they started talking, Archie knew that Curtis wasn't crazy. Everything he said made sense. He took the book, *Bahá'u'lláh and the New Era*, that Curtis gave him and went home, vowing to read it. Several days elapsed before he opened the book after supper one night. At 2:00 A.M. he closed the book, rushed into the bedroom to share the good news with his wife Agnes, that he had found what he had always been searching for. Half asleep and irritated, Agnes thought, 'Not again!' When he continued to enthuse like someone who had discovered a new love, Archie's wife sat up in bed and said angrily, 'Archie, if you join one more thing, I'll leave you.' Archie replied, 'Well, you'll just have to leave then, because this is the truth.'

Archie ended his search, becoming a Bahá'í. About a year later, after varied attempts to interest Agnes in the Faith, she too became a Bahá'í. It wasn't what he said that convinced her. It was the change in Archie, and meeting people like Curtis that drew her into the embrace of Bahá'u'lláh. (Also, the fact that Archie could drop out of Masonry was a signal to her that he was certain he would never search for another religious, ideological or philosophical organization again.)

For forty-nine years Archie never missed a Feast, served on several Assemblies, was a delegate to the national Bahá'í convention for many years, and with Curtis pioneered the development of the audio-visual department for the National Spiritual Assembly.

Even during those desperate days of the Depression, Curtis understood the need to preserve every historic aspect of the Cause in New Jersey. He persuaded Archie and Agnes to give up their house, which they had difficulty paying for, and move instead into a house in Teaneck where 'Abdu'l-Bahá stayed in 1912. By helping the believer who lived there to meet her mortgage payments, the Tichenors would keep that historically significant property in Bahá'í hands.

The Depression hurt almost everyone in the country, even the Continental Pipe Manufacturing Company. There were very few calls for building pipelines. Some repair jobs, but that was about all. So Curtis couldn't count on his father's business to help him provide even the bare necessities of life for his family. He persevered as a local electrician. Times were so tight that for several years meat was served only once a week in Curtis' and Harriet's home – and that was one pound of hamburger. Candy? Only once in a while. But despite battling daily to keep from caving in economically, the Kelseys always contributed to the Bahá'í Fund. Curtis didn't do that out of duty, or expecting to be rewarded for the act of giving. If Bahá'u'lláh, 'Abdu'l-Bahá and Shoghi Effendi stressed the importance of contributing to the Fund, then there was absolutely no question about giving; it was an act of love. Giving to the Fund gave him as much joy as teaching. His children knew that, and as adults they adopted the same attitude. Of course, there were those, even some Bahá'ís, who tried to discourage Curtis from being so generous in the light of his economic circumstances.

Being poor produced pain; but it was the kind of ache that Curtis could take, because he was certain that eventually he would free his family from poverty's hold. Something was going to happen, something he couldn't spell out – an unheralded business opportunity, perhaps, an intriguing job offer. It wouldn't be something he could find in the classified ads. Something was going to happen that would change his family's economic condition. How? Where? When? He couldn't say. All he knew was that the feeling he had was real. Yet Curtis didn't wait in a rocking-chair for opportunity to strike through a celestial bolt. He did what the Teachings urge believers to do. He worked hard, trying to build his electricity business, doing the best job he could. Whether he succeeded, depended on God's Will. He prayed daily for assistance; and he didn't feel self-conscious about doing that, because he wasn't concerned about making a million dollars in order to gain high social status and power to impress people. All he wanted was to be able to feed his family without being anxious about where the next meal was going to come from. To Curtis, praying for economic help was sensible. After all, he reasoned, if you believe that God is all-loving, all-caring and all-knowing and you don't seek His help, you are like a person standing near a fire extinguisher and not using it while watching your car burn up. He believed that God is a loving father, who provides His children with what He thinks they need. He was certain God answered his prayers.

There were times when Curtis and Harriet went to bed

knowing they didn't have enough food to feed their children adequately the next day, and in the morning would find sacks of food on their front doorstep. The bundles were always dropped off anonymously. As adults, the Kelsey children learned the names of some of those anonymous donors.

Though materially poor, Curtis never allowed his spirit to become impoverished. He was essentially happy.

His optimism shielded his family from the reach of gloom, which had invaded almost every home in Teaneck during the Great Depression. For most people, the future seemed bleak, at best, fuzzy. It seemed as if people had given up on the economic system and didn't know where to turn for a replacement. Though the prevailing condition affected Curtis and Harriet at times, it never overwhelmed them so they lost their special spiritual perspective. In fact, despite the difficulty of earning enough money each week, they understood that the Great Depression was a phase of God's plan to establish a world society based on justice. Knowing he and his family were part of that process helped to dull the ache of poverty. The family adjusted to the lack of money, but never so much that they felt they could never catapult out of that condition into a more affluent situation. To Curtis the future always looked bright. Because of that attitude Curtis did things that people in his economic condition usually never did. He would take his family to the Green Acre Bahá'í School in Eliot, Maine, even to the Louhelen School in Davison, Michigan, always traveling by car and sleeping in it, or in a tent. Hotels, of course, were out of the question. At Green Acre they couldn't afford to stay at the Inn, which in those days was operated like a fancy country club, with doilies on the tables and uniformed waitresses. Despite the smart setting, the Kelseys attended classes and participated in the recreation programs, such as swimming in the river, hiking and picking berries. They never felt different from those who were living at the Inn. Curtis put up a tent where the family slept, washed, cooked, ate their meals and battled mosquitos fiercer than the Teaneck variety. It was a precious experience, something the children still cherish.

Meeting Louis Gregory enriched their lives. Awed by Mr Gregory, the children considered him the 'sage of the age,' a title they never shared with him, but which everyone in the children's school approved of. Every time they visited Green Acre in the late 1930s and 1940s, Harriet and Curtis made sure the children met Louis Gregory. Before going to his home, the children were scrubbed, and dressed in their best clothing. They didn't remember what Mr Gregory told them. That wasn't as important, their parents felt, as being exposed to the brilliant spirit of the man.

While at Green Acre they met other outstanding people and basked in a spirit they could experience nowhere else during the rest of the year. There, they came to know people from all over the world, played with the kinds of youngsters they would never meet in Teaneck. In a sense, by being in Green Acre every summer, Curtis, Harriet and the children gained a better understanding of what the Bahá'í Civilization would be like. Everyone grew from their Green Acre experience. But what they gained could not be measured through established testing means. How do you scientifically gauge the development of the soul, an intangible, unseeable force? The children learned some basic facts of the Faith, but what they learned by simply being at the Bahá'í school was far more valuable.

Curtis didn't take his children to Green Acre because taking them there was part of some educational plan he had devised. He knew very little about what constitutes a good educational curriculum. He and his family went because Shoghi Effendi urged believers to attend Bahá'í summer schools. If the Guardian felt it was the right thing to do then it had to be done, regardless of the circumstances and obstacles in the way. There was no question in Curtis' mind that his children, in fact all children, would benefit from their Green Acre experience. He believed that with all his heart and soul.

For most children in America, growing up during the Great Depression was difficult. The pressures their parents felt were unwittingly passed on to them. There was so much that children wanted, but couldn't get. It got so bad, that denial became routine. Curtis and Harriet were concerned that their children should not grow up with a deprivation complex. One way of preventing that from happening was for father to take one or two of the children on his business trips during the summer time. The plan worked. Only June had difficulty; she was prone to car sickness.

Often the trips would take two or three days, sometimes longer. They would camp out and wash in a stream; and there was always a stop at an ice-cream stand for a large cone. At times there were two or three stops. Curtis had a passion for ice cream; and the children knew it. On these trips, he derived pleasure from showing the children the pipelines he and their grandfather had built throughout New England, New York State and Pennsylvania. And they were impressed that their father had built such big things.

There was a certain kind of spirit on those trips that made going with 'Pop' fun. On the road, Curtis was buoyant and energetic, because he was a natural roamer, an incurable adventurer. On a trip the day was full of promise; he was in his car, and over the hill at the next stop there was the strong possibility that he was going to secure work, maybe a big contract. Even after a rejection, there was always the next hill to climb. Curtis always made sure to visit with the Bahá'ís along the way; and that was fun for the children, because they would sometimes meet other Bahá'í children and friendships developed. And there was always the chance of being offered chocolates, something they were rarely allowed at home.

On these trips they also got to see a side of their father they weren't aware of at home: that was his happy-go-lucky spirit, which they could relate to, because it was childlike. Sitting behind the steering-wheel, driving down a country road, Curtis would often sing songs, actually original tunes with senseless lyrics he would make up on the spot. He would sing full-blast, phrases like, 'Cool, Clear Water,' over and over again. Another favorite of his was 'Lolly pop, polly lop.'

Sometimes he would break into a more traditional musical mode, singing 'Home, Home on the Range,' no doubt an expression of his life-long yearning to return to the west. There were times when Curtis would take the whole family on one of these trips in his black 1932 Buick. In the big trunk was a tent, other camping gear and food. It was a fun time, lots of singing, laughter, story-telling, pranks, and playful teasing. And Curtis was the most notorious tease. He would look into the car's rear view mirror to see who was preoccupied, then tap that child on the shoulder; then, when the child wondered who had been responsible, he would pretend to know nothing about it. Watching the children accusing each other generated a childish glee in Curtis. After a while he would confess, and break into laughter. And his laughter would set the rest of the family laughing.

When Curtis called on a prospective client, Harriet would start a round of prayers. Usually the longer the interview the greater the chance of securing business. The exciting time was watching Curtis returning to the car. Grinning meant he had been successful. So everyone would strain to see if Pop was at least smiling, for that could mean the firm was leaning toward doing business with Continental Pipe Manufacturing Company.

On one of these outings the children received an unforgettable lesson on the power of prayer. The family had been on the road in New England for two weeks, stopping at power and water companies and not obtaining any positive responses. To make matters worse, Curtis was running low on money. In fact, he didn't have enough to return to Teaneck. The only uplifting periods of time were spent with the Bahá'ís along the way.

One night, after another disappointing day, Curtis was looking for a place to camp. The spot he found seemed ideal. No thorny bushes or trees to block the view of the star-filled sky; and the pleasant breeze was a relief from the hot, humid day on the road. But around dawn, some of the children got up earlier than usual, for the stench permeating the tent was horrible. When they dashed out and quickly surveyed the area they discovered they had camped on the edge of a town garbage and junk dump. Evidently, the breeze had shifted during the night. It didn't take long to pack up and get out of that place.

Perhaps in his haste to leave, Curtis had not tied the tent securely onto the back of the car, for it fell off while he was driving. When he retrieved it, it was ruined, full of large holes. What a dilemma! Only enough money for a few more meals and now no overnight shelter. And he had to be on the road for another five days, because there were more scheduled business calls to make. Though the family prayed every day, they prayed harder after losing the tent. Curtis believed God would answer his plea for help. How? He didn't know. But he was sure God would answer.

Back on the road, and after two unsuccessful stops, Curtis started hunting for a place to spend the night, a place that would protect his family from the elements. He finally found a spot – a gully with a clear stream. In a matter of minutes, Curtis had a fire going, and Harriet scraped up enough food for the family's last hot meal. While cooking, she asked the children to wash for supper, and they scampered to the stream. On the way they discovered six or seven colorful objects on the ground with a lot of quarters around them. They were machines, and as they pulled the knobs more coins shot out of them. Mary Louise rushed back to her folks with a handful of quarters and explained what they had found.

Curtis got enough money from the abandoned gambling-casino slot-machines to buy a tent and not have to worry about food and gasoline for the remainder of the trip. But the Kelseys' sudden good fortune didn't end with the discovery of a pot-of-cash; Curtis secured a contract to build a pipeline from the last business he called on.

On January 4, 1932 Curtis' father passed away after an illness that affected every bodily function. Only his mind remained sound until the day he died. A few days before his father's death, Curtis visited with him, and because of what transpired at the bedside he didn't grieve when he learned about his father's passing.

Curtis never forgot that moment when he sat beside his father, looking into his fading eyes and hearing him whisper with assurance, 'I'm now sure there is a life after this one – I know.' Hearing that made Curtis happy not only because his father's stubborn resistance to a basic truth had caved in, and he had become enlightened on such an essential matter, but that his personal relationship with his father had become closer. With the acceptance of the immortality of the soul, Frank Kelsey, Curtis sensed, had also accepted Bahá'u'lláh. In the next world, Curtis believed, there would be a wholehearted reunion with his father.

But several weeks later, when he read the will, he couldn't believe the document. He was dumbstruck. In his will, Frank Kelsey left the greatest share of his estate, including his company, to his widow. To Curtis, his father's decision was cruel as well as unjust. When he thought seriously about his family's predicament and what the will stated, Curtis fumed. Marjorie was to gain control of a company she was unprepared to head. Curtis didn't expect a handout. He would have rejected that, even though it would have assured more groceries for the family. But how could his father have ignored all that he had done to help the company develop? He had been brought up in a home where hydraulic engineering talk was common. Designing and building water, power and sewer systems was perfectly natural for Curtis. He enjoyed the business, as opposed to his brothers Arthur and Robert. But there was nothing Curtis could do immediately. Though he sensed that Marjorie wanted to sell her shares of the company, he didn't have the capital to purchase them, and securing a bank loan was impossible considering his economic condition. And what if she got a buyer?

Curtis brooded. That feeling that something good was going to happen wasn't as strong as it had been. In fact, at times it wasn't noticeable at all. He had prayed fervently for Divine help, and now he was faced with a setback he hadn't anticipated. It was difficult not thinking about his father's will. He felt betrayed, angry at Marjorie, because he suspected that she had persuaded Frank Kelsey to change his will while he was on his sickbed. The court stated that the will was dated only a month before Mr Kelsey's passing. And Curtis knew his father had made out a will much earlier than that date. He was sure his father, under normal circumstances, would never agree to his wife possessing the majority of the company's stock. What he could do as head of Continental Pipe! he thought. And in that position, he would be able to provide his family with the things they needed. Curtis even wondered if God had heard his prayers, was aware of his needs. He couldn't remember when he had felt worse.

While alone and close to breaking-point, Haifa came to mind, then 'Abdu'l-Bahá's face. It was a repeat of those precious moments in the Master's room on that sunny autumn afternoon in 1921. 'Abdu'l-Bahá was looking at him, more than that, peering into his soul. Depression's grip loosened, and that good feeling returned; and with that, understanding of why he was being tested. Detachment – that's what he had to learn. Putting his trust in God before all else, doing His bidding first and not relying on the contingent world for happiness and security. With that, he realized, he would find contentment.

While Curtis struggled to earn a living from his electrical shop, his brother Arthur tried to run the company for

Marjorie. But that arrangement failed. Arthur was more interested in charting horoscopes than hunting for business. Besides, during the Depression the power and water companies had no desire to build new pipelines. Only a disaster could force them to change their position. With no work, the subsidy agreement Continental Pipe had with a Seattle-based lumber company was in danger of being ended. It was the money the company received from the west coast that helped to pay the rent for the company's offices. Arthur grew depressed, for he was witnessing the demise of a company his father had made flourish. Failure even to make the business meet its costs, plus not being able to earn a decent livelihood for his wife Olivia, brought alive the memory of his father's pronouncement 'that he would never amount to anything.' Arthur quit Continental, and when Marjorie passed away, Curtis took over the business and opened his home to Arthur and his wife, who lived there for more than a year, not having to pay rent.

One day Arthur announced that he had worked out a horoscope, predicting the day of his death. Because he was sure he was right, he bought a large life assurance policy. At least Olivia would benefit financially from his death, something he couldn't arrange while alive. The day of Arthur's self-predicted death arrived and he didn't even have a sniffle, so he canceled the insurance. The next day Arthur dropped dead.

Curtis was shaken by the loss of his older brother. Though they had their differences, he loved Arthur. The fact that Arthur never realized his potential saddened Curtis. If only his father had recognized Arthur's creative and analytical qualities and encouraged him to develop them, he would

have lived longer, Curtis believed. He was convinced that
Arthur wanted to end his existence in a world where he had
experienced very little happiness.

A grief-stricken Curtis took over the business, knowing
that only Bahá'u'lláh's assistance would help him succeed.
But there wasn't much to work with, except a good
reputation that his father had built over the years.
Fortunately, Arthur and Marjorie didn't have much
opportunity to discredit the company, because they were
unable to solicit much business.

The first thing Curtis did was rehire the secretary who had
worked for his father. Her knowledge of the business was
solid; in fact, she was more like an administrative aide. With
her in the Woolworth Building office, he was going to spend
most of his time knocking on potential clients' doors, even if
the nation was still gripped by a deep depression. Though
naturally shy, circumstances made him into an appealing
salesman. He was tired of living on the edge of poverty.
Something had to be done to make life more comfortable,
more secure for his family. With that incentive, Curtis
pursued clients doggedly. Also Curtis' natural stubbornness
helped him to persist. And the persistence paid off; he began
to obtain small repair orders. The money he received from
that was more lucrative than from his electrical shop. So
Curtis closed the store, investing all of his professional energy
and time in re-establishing Continental Pipe.

After obtaining a job, he would go into the field to direct
the work crew, which was made up of veteran Maine
lumbermen, whose language was heavily streaked with
vulgarities, and who enjoyed whiskey and brawling. Strength
was what they respected most. Because Curtis was able to

wield a twenty-pound sledge hammer efficiently, they accepted him as their leader.

Even in the field, Curtis would work at night, putting together proposals to companies that invited Continental Pipe to bid on prospective jobs. During the first two years as head of the company, Curtis wasn't home much. Even when he was in Teaneck on weekends, a lot of his time was spent doing Bahá'í projects and repairing things around the house.

There was a time during this period when he felt his optimism had led him into a situation he couldn't handle. The repair job he had contracted to do turned out too complicated to complete. He sensed that when he first negotiated with the electrical company engineers. But that notion was quickly pushed aside by a more characteristic notion; once back at the office he would figure out how to solve the problem. But no amount of office reflection and pondering helped. He wasn't a traditionally trained engineer; with that kind of background, he thought, he could have done the job. What to do? He couldn't drop the job, not with the men in the field and supplies being delivered to the work site. Besides, word of Continental quitting a job because it wasn't capable of completing it would spread to most potential clients in the industry and his company would be stamped 'a loser.'

So Curtis did the only thing left for him to do: he prayed for assistance. And help came – in the form of a dream. After tossing and turning in bed one night, he finally fell into a restless sleep. Curtis' father came to him; and he came close, his cheek on Curtis' cheek. It was so real he could feel the breath of his father. And Frank Kelsey started talking, telling him how to handle the difficult project. The next day Curtis applied everything his father suggested, and he completed the job before he was supposed to. But that dream had more significance to Curtis than the imparting of instructions; it demonstrated to Curtis that his father had discovered his true self; that the hard-heartedness and anger that characterized his later years had been stripped away; that he was now able to share his love wholeheartedly with his son. Curtis felt that way, because in all the years he knew his father, he never placed his cheek against his.

During the trying Great Depression days, Curtis would sometimes say when he was in a dreamy state of mind and among family or close friends, 'I'm waiting for my ship to come in.' The children were so familiar with the statement that it didn't take long to figure out what he meant by it. It was Curtis' way of saying that he couldn't wait until he started making more money so he could do the things he always wanted to do.

Well, 1939 was the year when the 'ship started coming in.' After years of calling on the Nashua Paper Company in New Hampshire, that firm approached Continental Pipe, asking for a large pipeline to be built. But this time Curtis couldn't be in the field, because other companies were approaching him to bid on forthcoming jobs. So he assembled the usual crew of Maine lumbermen, drew up the construction plans and decided to visit the work site on weekends.

Unfortunately, not everything worked out the way he hoped it would. Though he had a good rapport with the lumbermen, the timekeeper, who was young and unyielding, was unable to communicate effectively with the workers. In fact, some contemplated killing him. At one point, some of the workers were so outraged, they dumped expensive tools into the river. After that incident, control broke down; and some of the specially treated wood, the basic pipe material, which had been shipped from the west coast, started disappearing. It was obvious that someone was stealing the wood staves.

Curtis had to leave his office and rush up to New Hampshire. One of the first things he did was replace the timekeeper with a more mature man, Donald Kinney, a Bahá'í from Teaneck. In a few days, Donald was able to restore order and direct a successful tool-finding expedition. With the help of the local police, Curtis uncovered the whereabouts of the wood. A local farmer had taken the material during the course of several nights and used it to build a bridge over a stream on his property so his cattle could move more easily from pasture to pasture. When Curtis confronted the farmer, he didn't demand that he return the wood. In fact, Curtis didn't make an issue of it, because he noticed how poor the man was and how downtrodden his family was.

The police chief was surprised that Curtis didn't press charges against the farmer. When others, including Donald Kinney, heard that Curtis hadn't taken any action against the farmer they were surprised, because they knew Curtis was a stickler for principle. In fact, Donald remembered his own father, Saffa Kinney, being taken before the Local Spiritual Assembly by Curtis, who alleged that Mr Kinney claimed that 'Abdu'l-Bahá was a prophet. Curtis did this despite his respect and admiration for Mr Kinney, whom the Master had called 'one of the pillars of the Faith in America.' The Saffa Kinney case was a painful experience, because he loved Mr Kinney. But he did what had to be done. His detachment was

so pronounced in Bahá'í circles, that Curtis proved to be a
test to many Bahá'ís who thought of him as unfeeling and
unyielding. Curtis had faith in the Assembly's decision, that
only good would result from it; he didn't view the Assembly
as an inquisitional court, but rather, as a trustworthy
dispenser of justice, and believed that everyone, including
Mr Kinney, would benefit from the Assembly's decision.
Curtis' daughter June has always felt that one of her father's
most admirable qualities was his ability to disassociate a
wrongful act from the perpetrator. Because of that, he never
held a grudge, or grew to dislike someone because of a
particular action committed by that person.

Though Curtis had succeeded in restoring Continental
Pipe Manufacturing Company to a healthy business, the
Kelseys didn't change much of their life-style. They
continued to go where they wanted to go, but instead of
camping or sleeping in the car, they spent nights in hotels. He
continued to drive a Buick, but a new one instead of an old
one. And Harriet got her own car. With more money
available Curtis and Harriet automatically increased their
contribution to the Fund. They purchased new furniture,
even got a legitimate couch for the parlor, long enough, of
course, to squeeze five seekers on it instead of four for their
weekly firesides. And their house continued to be open to
those who needed a place to stay overnight; and there were
those who came for one night and stayed thirty, sometimes
longer. Bob, Curtis' youngest brother, and his wife were
frequent visitors. At one time they spent more than a year,
always staying rent-free. It was Curtis' way of helping his
brother get started professionally without having the burden
of paying heavy living expenses. The trouble was that Bob

never got a successful professional start and eventually became an alcoholic, and turned cynical. Curtis had hoped that by living in a Bahá'í home Bob would grow to love the Faith and embrace it. Though his wife became a Bahá'í, Bob fought it, very much like his father. In fact, there were times when he would ridicule the Faith in Curtis' presence without ever succeeding in upsetting his brother, which, for some reason, he wanted desperately to do. Often when going to a local saloon, he would invite Curtis to come along for a drink or two, even though he knew that as a Bahá'í Curtis didn't partake of alcoholic beverages. But here again Bob failed to provoke Curtis whose usual response was either laughter or stony-faced silence. Seeing his brother degenerate hurt Curtis, not only because he knew how much potential Bob had and that he was wasting it, but because his mother was always concerned about Bob's future, his character-development. In some respects, Curtis felt that Bob's failure in life was his fault.

Harriet's mother came to live with the Kelseys in the dark days of the Depression when food was scarce. How could Curtis say no to her request since her other children, who were in better financial circumstances than he was, said they couldn't afford to have her? Grandma Morgan became a delightful part of the family, a tiny, plucky lady, possessing a rich reservoir of epigrams and a sharp wit. What also made her exciting was her unpredictable manner. One day a six-year-old girl asked her how old she was; 'Oh, I guess I'm sixty or seventy,' she responded, without batting an eye. She was in her eighties at the time. Grandma Morgan, who had been a confirmed Baptist, accepted Bahá'u'lláh about ten years before she passed away at the age of ninety-three.

Harriet's sister Edith and brother-in-law Perry, a noted landscape artist and art critic, lived for several winters with the Kelseys. Living in New Hampshire's mountains was too cold. Through their experiences in Teaneck both Edith and Perry became Bahá'ís. Though they didn't pay for their stay, Perry gave Curtis painting lessons, which turned out to be an illuminating experience, because he learned he had talent. Curtis continued to paint late into his life. His most prized work was a portrait of 'Abdu'l-Bahá, which hangs in the parlor of his daughter Carol's home.

Not only family members came to stay with the Kelseys, even during the Depression. Other people, Bahá'í and non-Bahá'í, gravitated toward that odd, little pink house that seemed out of place in the typical American suburban setting. John Marlowe, a fiery poet, who had little formal education and who leaned toward Communism before becoming a Bahá'í, found the Kelsey home open to him. He stayed there because he felt genuinely welcome. Having been an orphan, he had grown up sensitive to whether he was truly accepted or not. Much of the time he was rejected. The happy spirit of the home touched him. So did Curtis' attitude toward him. Curtis was never suspicious of him, something that was difficult for John to understand. No one ever trusted him so. Curtis' confidence in John helped him to gain confidence in himself. The incident that impressed him the most was when Curtis asked him to follow his car in an old truck to a distant garage on the other side of town. John had driven little, and he had no license; but he hopped into the truck and after much grinding of gears took after Curtis through traffic and over bridges to the final destination. After that, John had a lot more confidence in his ability to drive.

And John never forgot all the moral support Curtis gave him during the days he was baking bread at the Kelseys and trying to sell it in the neighborhood.

In the thirty years the Kelseys lived in Teaneck, hundreds of people visited them. It is true that some guests took advantage of their hospitality, sometimes borrowing money and never paying it back. But that didn't discourage them from keeping their home open to all. No other house in the neighborhood attracted so many different kinds of people. It was like a branch of the United Nations. Blacks, American Indians, Chinese, Latins, Tongans, Africans, Jews, Christians, Muslims, Hindus, atheists, old and young, poor and rich, were drawn to the Kelseys. Mrs Zam of New York City, an older Jewish lady, whose daughter was a Bahá'í and who had learned to love Curtis and Harriet, would show up at the house with her trusty shopping bag at the oddest hours. She came usually to drink in the kind of spirit that she couldn't find anywhere else. Perhaps it was that happy spirit that John always felt. Often she would stay for supper and share in the spare servings.

Grace Krug who was living with her wealthy sister after the death of her husband, Dr Krug, would come to Teaneck in a chauffeur-driven car to spend several days with Curtis and his family. Every time she came she would bring boxes of food, including a few chickens. Being with the Kelseys, even with their wicker furniture and drafty walls, was a lot more exciting than her sister's stuffy mansion in Rye, New York. To her, the spirit of 'Abdu'l-Bahá was in Curtis' home.

Even Curtis' daughters' friends found the house had a special attraction. His daughter Carol remembers when one of her old boy friends, who was now married and unaware

that Carol was around, came to visit the Kelseys on his way
through town with his family. He wanted to return to a place
that always made him feel at ease and joyful. He was the
same young man who told Curtis one day when he was
visiting Carol that his ambition was to own a liquor store.
Though Carol remembers her father not gulping or twitching,
he didn't greet the news with enthusiasm. On the other hand,
he didn't try to dissuade the young man from pursuing his
career goal. His response was the familiar stony-faced
silence, a posture he assumed whenever he felt negative
about something and didn't want to say anything that would
hurt the other person's feelings.

Over the years the Kelsey children were treated to a
parade of prominent Bahá'ís who came to spend some time at
their home. Open to the memoriam section of any *Bahá'í
World* volume: most Americans listed there were guests at
Curtis' home. So many – Lua Getsinger and her husband,
Louis Gregory, May Maxwell, Albert Windust, the Kinneys,
Horace Holley, Leroy Ioas, Mary Hanford Ford, Martha
Root, Amelia Collins, Keith Ransom-Kehler, Genevieve
Coy, Harlan Ober, Hooper Harris, Matthew Bullock,
Winston Evans, Howard McNutt, Fred Schophlocher,
George Spendlove, Dorothy Baker, Kenneth Christian, and
others. They came even during the Depression. Perhaps they
too sensed the spirit of 'Abdu'l-Bahá in the Kelsey home.

As soon as you entered the Kelsey home, you felt
something pleasantly different. It was a home that was used –
every part of it – but used lovingly. Even when Curtis was
prospering economically, the home was never lavishly
decorated. It was a physically comfortable place to be; but it
wasn't the chairs, sofa and lamps that you noticed. What was

more striking was 'The Greatest Name' hanging on the living room wall, pictures of 'Abdu'l-Bahá, the Bahá'í books and the spirit of genuine welcome which everybody sensed as they entered the home, even people of different cultures.

Meals at the Kelseys were always exciting for the children, because they never knew who would be coming by for lunch or dinner. It could be a Hand of the Cause of God or a new believer, a seeker, a wealthy entrepreneur or an unemployed man and his family. The conversation was always stimulating, and usually punctuated with laughter, and some aspect of the Faith would invariably be brought up. At the time, the children couldn't fully appreciate what everyone, including themselves, gained from such conversation. Only later in life did they realise that their parents' dining room was a learning center, in some respects like the dining room where the Master and His guests ate.

As a relatively early believer in the United States, Curtis experienced the start of the establishment of Bahá'u'lláh's Administrative Order. It was a trying time, for things were done by well-meaning people, even highly respected people, that were counter to the spirit and letter of Bahá'í administration. Watching members of an Assembly compromising with principles or dragging prevailing political procedures into Assembly deliberations, irked Curtis. And he wasn't afraid to share his feelings with the Assembly. His passion for abiding by principle was so strong that many Bahá'ís considered him strong-willed and hard-headed.

There was a time when no member of the Teaneck Assembly would speak to Curtis, and they even shunned him for a year. But he attended every Assembly meeting and Feast. Attending these gatherings was painful. Had he not been a Bahá'í, he would never have endured the attempt to ostracize him. It was only his love for the Faith and his understanding of what the Administrative Order would one day become – a mighty framework for the Kingdom of God on Earth – that kept him from fleeing from the situation. He had to be patient – like the Master. Unity had to be maintained at all costs. Eventually the matter that led to the estrangement between Curtis and the other members of the Assembly was settled. Everyone was speaking to him again, and there were those who appreciated Curtis' steadfastness, because it taught them a lesson in firmness in the Covenant of Bahá'u'lláh.

Many years later Polly Marlowe learned from Curtis the wisdom of maintaining unity when she served on an Assembly in the South: 'He helped us with love and good sense to be better Bahá'ís – in our inner life, in our community life, or on our Assemblies. One instance of this has been a guide through the years: I was troubled because an Assembly we served on seemed to be planning things contrary to the Teachings, yet when I voiced an opinion the warm spiritual atmosphere of the Assembly seemed to crack with ice. I asked Curtis what to do in such a situation, and he pointed out that if an opinion causes disunity, in most cases it is important to lay aside your opinion and go along with the majority in order to preserve the unity of the whole. Soon after this advice had been given, the Assembly, in setting up a public meeting, decided that the publicity should not say "open to all races." Because this Assembly was in the South this meant (at that time) the friends from the black race would not think they were welcome. I was disturbed but wholly gave up my opinion to the majority decision. The next

day the publicity was taken to the newspaper and very shortly
after this, the newspaper called our chairman to ask if all
races were welcome, and could this be stated, to which the
chairman replied, "Yes." The meeting turned out to be a
success.'

Chapter 12

Curtis never forgot his formal school experiences, because they were painful. He felt like a prisoner in a classroom. Consequently, he harbored a distrust for the world of academe, something never expressed publicly, but shared with people close to him. Because of his unpleasant encounter with school, and because of his ability to become a hydraulic engineer through personal initiative, he felt that higher education was a waste of time, energy and money, with the exception of medicine, law and the technologies. He didn't discourage people from pursuing university degrees; but on the other hand he didn't encourage them to further their education. This was true with his children, who had a strong capacity for learning.

But though in his lifetime none of his children were university graduates, they were all active explorers of knowledge, continually reading Bahá'í and non-Bahá'í material and engaging in lively intellectual discussions. Their healthy appetite for knowledge and active pursuit of it wasn't something they inherited. It was learned, mainly from their father, who was a serious student of the Teachings.

As children, they remember Curtis reading and making notes, talking to them about different aspects of the Revelation and enthusiastically sharing certain insights he had gained from his reading. Those were exciting times, because the children's minds and hearts were opened to weighty topics like 'life after death,' 'soul, mind and spirit,' 'free will and predestination.' As an adult he rarely missed a day or night reading from the sacred texts. It got so that he would feel uncomfortable if he forgot to read. His wasn't a fanatical attachment to the Writings; it was a love affair. How could a lover stay away from his beloved? The Writings were the source of his strength, his well-being; through them he gained understanding of the meaning of life; he discovered happiness. If it provided all of that, he reasoned, he would be a fool to neglect reading the utterances of Bahá'u'lláh and 'Abdu'l-Bahá. But although he enjoyed his private moments with the Creative Word, he began reading because Bahá'u'lláh urged the believers to do it. To Curtis, it made sense to do what the Manifestation of God asks or commands, for you could only benefit by complying.

Often in a Bahá'í study class or Feast, people, including those who were highly educated, would turn to Curtis for answers to complicated questions. In responding, he never adopted a superior air or slipped into self-righteousness. Answers were always given in the spirit of sharing and service. Perhaps that's why so many people felt comfortable asking him questions. Though it was apparent he knew a lot about the Revelation, he wasn't perceived as a 'know-it-all.' Curtis was approachable, because people sensed his genuine desire to serve them.

Despite his lack of literary training, Curtis became an effective editor. He loved searching the Writings and putting together compilations on various topics. His search would take him through old books, journals, magazines and newspapers. Almost every Bahá'í book in English in the world was in his library, as well as a set of *Star of the West*, Mírzá Abu'l-Faḍl's *Bahá'í Proofs* and *Brilliant Proofs*, *Maḥmúd's Diary*, almost every copy of *World Order* magazine (the 1930s and 1940s set) and a complete *Bahá'í News* file.

Many a night was spent in his office above the garage, combing through the treasury of Bahá'u'lláh and 'Abdu'l-Bahá's Writings. To him there was nothing more thrilling, because of what he discovered. Unearthing something new, gaining deeper insight into passages he had read before, generated childlike wonderment in him. He couldn't wait to share what he had found with the family.

Word regarding Curtis' compilations reached many of the Bahá'ís of northern New Jersey, and he was encouraged to make them available to the friends. So Curtis started printing tracts on love, peace, justice, the oneness of humankind, the Covenant, often with pictures of 'Abdu'l-Bahá. The contents came strictly from the Sacred Writings. He made charts on subjects like progressive revelation. What he produced was tastefully done; the text was usually printed on colored paper, and the passages were spaced in an easy-to-read arrangement. Many of Curtis' tracts were circulated by the friends, reaching places in the south, midwest and far west, and providing inspiration and spiritual perspective to many believers. His production of tracts was motivated by a desire to help the believers gain a better understanding of the Faith.

Over the years, Curtis received many letters of appreciation for the printed materials he produced at no cost to the friends.

Curtis scrutinized non-Bahá'í literature as well, not for reading enjoyment, but rather, to find information that would support the Bahá'í view. He clipped newspapers and magazines regularly. He lifted passages from books, dealing with human behavior, world affairs, metaphysics, the origin of the universe. His files bulged with non-Bahá'í quotations. Curtis did this because Shoghi Effendi had urged the believers, through pilgrims' notes, to read non-Bahá'í material so they would gain a better grasp of contemporary life. By doing this, Curtis found that he was able to speak to groups on a variety of topics, from economics and science and religion, to Biblical prophecies and reincarnation. From his collection of both Bahá'í and non-Bahá'í quotations, Curtis created what his children called 'Pop's Bible.' Through the years this notebook, which had fifteen categories, grew thicker. Meditation and prayer; the fear of God; evolution; nearness to God; free will; mind, soul and spirit, obedience, and backbiting: these were some of the categories. While compiling that notebook, he was putting together another one, which emphasized the most likely questions that Bahá'ís would be asked by inquirers. The answers stemmed from a variety of Bahá'í books and non-Bahá'í sources. Curtis became so attached to the two notebooks that he never forgot to take them along on teaching and deepening trips. Often a tricky question at a fireside would move Curtis to delve into one of his notebooks.

Curtis also became famous in northeastern United States and Canada for his carefully thought-out and illustrated study class outlines. Somehow they reached scores of communities, stimulating and enlightening many people.

To Curtis, religion was the most intriguing topic of conversation. Even hydraulic engineering took second place. Politics usually put him to sleep. When he was engaged in a discussion on religion there was little chance of Curtis growing bored. He never could give a satisfactory answer as to why he enjoyed talking about religion. But those who knew him well understood how deep his commitment was to the Faith. Therefore, they reasoned, anything related to it would draw his attention. He particularly enjoyed talking religion with non-Bahá'ís, but not to win an argument or crush an opponent – that sort of thinking or desire was not part of Curtis' make-up. Instead, he viewed such a situation as an opportunity to teach, and as in his talks, his manner was genuine, never resorting to bombast, trickery, sarcasm and verbal ploys designed to embarrass. His sincerity and purity were disarming. As a result people who held strong convictions about their own religious beliefs listened to Curtis with genuine interest, even passionate adherents of Christian sects who went door-to-door trying to convert people.

One afternoon two Jehovah's Witnesses called on Curtis. He greeted them warmly and invited them inside, making them feel at ease. After praising them for their courage in breaking away from orthodoxy and expressing admiration for their devotion to their Faith, the two men relaxed. Then Curtis listened to what they had to say, much of it being read from the Bible they were holding. About ten minutes elapsed when Curtis said gently, 'Do you recall what is stated in the Book of Daniel? "Go thy way, Daniel, for the words are

ABOVE: Curtis and
Harriet camping.
BELOW: Roy Wilhelm,
Curtis and 'Al'áí
Kalántar on a camping
trip.

TOP LEFT: Curtis (at the steering wheel) with Roy Wilhelm.

BOTTOM LEFT: Interior of Curtis' electrical shop, 1930.

ABOVE: Curtis speaking to his children in their living room in Teaneck, 1937.

RIGHT: Curtis conducting a class at Rice Lake Bahá'í School, Canada, 1946.

ABOVE: Curtis (standing on the ground with cap) supervising installation of water pump in Bahjí, 1952. LEFT: Curtis and Fujita reunited in 1968, in front of the Master's house in Haifa.

closed up and sealed till the time of the end.'"

'Where is that?' said one of the men, handing his Bible to Curtis. Curtis turned several pages and said, 'Here ... in Daniel ... twelfth chapter, ninth verse.'

After reading the passage, one of them said, 'What is the significance of this?'

'To me,' Curtis responded, 'that passage means that the Bible, the Gospel is sealed until the time of the end, and even Jesus Christ didn't know when the time of the end would take place. Only the Father knew.'

The two men looked at Curtis strangely, wondering what he was trying to tell them. 'This may seem harsh,' Curtis said, 'but as a good Christian you shouldn't be using the Bible to teach your Faith. It is sealed until the time of the end.'

Then Curtis proceeded to tell them the story of Bahá'u'lláh, that it was He who came 'in the Glory of the Father' to unseal the Words in the Bible; and that Bahá'u'lláh was living during the time the first Jehovah's Witnesses were expecting the Return of Christ. In a gentle and patient manner Curtis had turned the teachers into enthralled students.

In the eyes of many Bahá'ís, Curtis was an outstanding teacher. But being referred to as a teacher embarrassed Curtis, and this feeling didn't stem only from modesty, but also from a deep-seated sense of inferiority, which would surface at times when he was engaged in conversations with people who had attained prominence in intellectual circles. All that he knew, together with his yearning to know more, came from his belief in Bahá'u'lláh. When asked to speak about the Faith to either Bahá'í or non-Bahá'í audiences, Curtis relied primarily on the Teachings and secular sources to support the Bahá'í point of view. He didn't have a style or method. How he expressed himself was perfectly natural. He was completely without affectation. Consequently his purity and sincerity were strikingly obvious, even to some skeptics.

Curtis' talks were always easy-flowing, never ponderous. Audiences were usually left in a positive frame of mind, with a good feeling about the Faith. He had a knack of demonstrating how the Faith relates to pressing contemporary issues, often quoting authorities and statistics which he had noted from journals and books. Anecdotes and earthy analogies were often used. His talks were peppered with memorized quotations from Bahá'u'lláh and 'Abdu'l-Bahá. That was done because the Guardian had urged the friends to commit to memory the Writings of the Central Figures of the Faith, so that the Message be given in its purest form.

His fireside talks were flexible. He attempted to reach the needs of those seekers who were at the meeting. So he tried to find out their backgrounds and interests before speaking. Because he studied the Writings daily, he didn't have to spend much time preparing for a fireside talk. Right quotes came at the right time. In teaching, he prayed fervently to be used as a clear channel so that the true seekers he encountered would be touched by the spirit of Bahá'u'lláh. Often while being introduced to an audience, you would see Curtis' lips moving slightly – he was beseeching Bahá'u'lláh's assistance through the Greatest Name.

Many of those who heard Curtis speak at summer schools, firesides, public meetings and from the university podium, sensed that he was guided by a Divine force. Some of the words that passed from his lips even surprised him. One night after making a point in his talk, he started to laugh and exclaimed, 'That's a great idea!' referring to what he had just said. He shook his head in amazement and laughed again.

It is easy to understand why those who heard Curtis speak or even engaged in conversation with him, felt he was a distinguished teacher. Physically, he gave the impression of being the classical professorial archetype, even in his mid-thirties, when he had turned prematurely gray. Some felt he resembled the late British historian Arnold Toynbee. Curtis was tall, slender and slightly stooped, wearing a tie and shirt even when gardening or building a swing for his grandchildren. Though he had little formal schooling, his speech-pattern was correct, possessing sound syntax, undoubtedly influenced by his literate and articulate mother. He had a strong logical mind, and he was easy to follow. And because he had a pure yearning to communicate, he qualified his generalities, often resorting to analogies and anecdotes, many of them funny. Despite his commonsense approach to life, he was witty, especially in his talks.

Curtis had a rich baritone voice and when he spoke, he projected strength and assurance. When he stood before an audience, tall, white-haired, clear-eyed and obviously happy, you would never think that he had never finished elementary school. Later in life, he participated in discussion panels at Green Acre with Dr Stanwood Cobb, an eminent educator and author, physicist Charles Wragg, and the Russian inventor of the fluorescent light, Nicholas Janus, discussing weighty subjects. Whenever Cobb, Wragg and Janus propounded the theories of Einstein, Eddington, Marx or Bacon, Curtis would always zero in on the Bahá'í view, often quoting from the Writings. The panelists respected his spiritual insights on whatever they were discussing.

Curtis gave the impression of being a refined and learned man, but not because he tried to create such an image. (He wasn't that kind of person.) Curtis was what he was. Pretense was foreign to him. If people perceived him as an intellectual, then so be it. But when friends discovered Curtis' educational background some would stare at him in disbelief. Such an occurrence took place one Sunday afternoon on the lawn of Curtis' home in Teaneck. He and his good friend, Matthew Bullock, a distinguished Boston attorney and member of the National Spiritual Assembly of the United States, were strolling together, talking about the condition of the Faith in America. After a lull in the conversation, Matthew stopped and asked, 'Curtis, you never told me what university you graduated from.' Curtis smiled and looked at the tall Harvard Law School graduate, adviser to President Franklin Delano Roosevelt on Black-American Affairs, and Chairman of the Massachusetts Parole Board, and chuckled, 'The university of hard knocks.'

Though Curtis didn't consider himself an educator, evidently the Hands of the Cause of God in America felt differently, for he was appointed an Auxiliary Board Member, one of their deputies. News of the appointment startled Curtis, because the Auxiliary Board is part of the institution of the learned in Bahá'u'lláh's administrative order. He felt there were many people who knew more about the Faith than he did. The fact that Auxiliary Board members advise the Hands of the Cause troubled him, because he genuinely felt inadequate to do that. Maybe he was chosen because he thought that way, for in the Bahá'í Faith, humility is an essential element in the make-up of a wise person. In

'Abdu'l-Bahá's words, 'If thou art seeking everlasting glory choose humility in the path of the True One.'

For fifteen years Curtis served as an Auxiliary Board Member, first under Hand of the Cause Dhikru'lláh Khádem, then under the North American Continental Board of Counsellors. Counsellor Florence Mayberry knew how Curtis served the Faith:

'Curtis had the resilience of a youth, even though he was honoured by many years. His spontaneity, his enthusiasm and above all the spirit of 'Abdu'l-Bahá which he reflected constantly in his talks made him one of the most sought after speakers by youth. Indeed, he was so popular with the youth that sometimes we called him the "youth" member of the Auxiliary Board. It was beautiful to see the touching affection between Curtis and the young people. The Indian people, so sensitive to the spirit, loved him. In fact, all of us loved him. And we knew clearly that he was an historic figure ...'

We hear people say from time to time that God works in mysterious ways. Usually those who say it have had experiences that enable them to share that belief with others. Those who knew Curtis' background and attended the first National Education Conference, sponsored by the National Spiritual Assembly of the United States, witnessed at the conference God's wisdom, expressed as it sometimes is, with a twist.

Several hundred Bahá'ís, mostly professional educators – psychologists, psychiatrists, educational innovators, university professors, deans, medical doctors – gathered in Wilmette, Illinois, to explore education as it affects society in general and the Bahá'í Community in particular. Erudite men and women delivered scholarly papers; consultation reached a high level. But the mood changed when Dr Donald Streets asked speaker Dr Edward Carpenter if he could share with the group an important message, which he had just been handed.

Dr Streets announced that Curtis Kelsey had died earlier in the day. Not a soul stirred. Most of the assemblage knew Curtis, appreciated and respected his knowledge. To them he was an outstanding teacher. Shaken, Dr Carpenter put his prepared text aside, and with tears streaming down his face, he related how Curtis Kelsey had guided him to Bahá'u'lláh. Fighting to control himself, a thought came to mind, which he had to share: 'Could we dedicate this conference on education to Curtis Kelsey?' he cried out. 'Yes,' was the overwhelming response.

Chapter 13

To Curtis, Shoghi Effendi was an extension of the Master, embodying many of His qualities and mannerisms. Curtis had known the Guardian fresh from Oxford University, and witnessed, to a degree, the shock that overcame Shoghi Effendi when it was revealed that he was named by his beloved Grandfather the Guardian of the Faith. He saw a change take place in Shoghi Effendi only a few days after the announcement was made; and he sensed, in Haifa, that when the Guardian returned from Switzerland the change would be even greater.

Curtis was right. He felt the change through the Guardian's writings. In a few months the lion cub had grown his mane and had become a mighty protector of the Cause of God. Curtis never doubted that Shoghi Effendi was being assisted by God; it was inconceivable to think otherwise. To Curtis, even Shoghi Effendi's writings were clear evidence of his special station in history. How Curtis loved Shoghi Effendi's writing. At times its majesty, power and sweep would take

Curtis' breath away. Obviously his devotion to Shoghi
Effendi impressed his children. They too accepted, without
question, as fact, that Shoghi Effendi was the 'sign of God' on
earth.

Curtis felt that Shoghi Effendi, like his Grandfather, had
the ability to sense the future, perceive the true feelings of
people, and gain special Divine assistance in working for the
Faith. The assistance was usually felt by those carrying out
Shoghi Effendi's assignments.

One day while Curtis was living in Teaneck, Curtis
received a letter from Shoghi Effendi's secretary, with a
check for $600, asking him to get the check to a certain
jeweler in New York City. The name of the jeweler was
given, but no address, home or office, was enclosed. Harriet
felt it was practically impossible to find the man, because he
had such a common name. When Curtis opened the
Manhattan borough phone book, he noticed the long listing
of identical last names. Not discouraged, he chose a number
and dialed it. When the party on the other end answered,
Curtis asked, 'Do you know His Eminence, Shoghi Effendi
Rabbani?'

'Yes, I do,' said the man.

That night Curtis was able to write to the Guardian that the
check had been delivered.

Roy Wilhelm and Curtis teamed up on another Holy Land
venture. It began innocently at Roy's new home in North
Lovell, Maine. 'The Shrine of the Báb area on Mount Carmel
needs a watering facility,' Roy said to Curtis. 'In fact, it was
the hope of the Master that one be constructed.' Roy
suggested that a water pump be installed, and that he would

pay for it. Roy asked Curtis if he would handle the project, because he had grown weary combating the cancer that had seized him.

The first thing Curtis had to do was purchase a water pump, which would cost $2,000. When he contacted Roy by phone to tell him what the pump cost, Roy was too ill to speak to him. Hebe Struven, a believer from nearby Freyburg, sister of Lua Getsinger, who was nursing Roy, told Curtis there was no money for the pump. It was difficult to believe what Hebe had told him, but he couldn't protest that Roy had promised to fund the project, because his long-time friend, and valiant servant of the Faith, was dying.

Concerned, Harriet wondered how Curtis was going to pay for the pump. In similar situations, he pointed out, Bahá'u'lláh had provided the means. Curtis borrowed the money from a bank, and had ninety days to pay it back. Two weeks later, Curtis received a phone call from Leroy Ioas, the Treasurer of the National Spiritual Assembly.

'Curtis,' he said, 'are you going to Haifa?'

'No – I have no plans to.'

'Well, the Guardian has asked us to send you a check for $10,000.'

Curtis chuckled to himself, as if to say, 'It works every time!' 'You better send me the check,' Curtis said, wondering why the extra $8,000.

The check was sent and Curtis opened a checking account in the name of the Guardian and himself. Soon after the money arrived, Curtis received a letter from the Guardian explaining what he wanted purchased: it was a lot more than the pump. Over the next few years Curtis had to purchase a pickup truck, an automobile, 3,000 feet of hose, cable-wiring, various fixtures and assorted odds and ends. To buy and ship everything the Guardian wanted, $40,000 more had to be deposited in the checking account.

Overseeing the supply needs of the Guardian as well as running his own company was taxing, so Curtis asked Donald Kinney to help with the purchasing. Buying the materials wasn't as difficult as shipping them, especially the big items. Curtis was dealing with a New Jersey-based shipping firm, the American Import and Export line. He never forgot that line, because of what was done to the brand new Ford pickup truck. When he came down to the wharf to watch the loading of the materials to Haifa, he was stunned to learn that the hubcaps, windshield-wipers, cigar-lighter, and glove-compartment light had been stripped from the vehicle. Incensed, he stormed into the office of the shipping line manager, demanding that the materials be replaced.

The man was extremely empathetic and then proceeded to explain the facts of life on America's coastal docks. Making an issue of the missing parts would only infuriate the longshoremen, he pointed out to Curtis, and in the end they would find a way of destroying the truck. Though steaming, Curtis accepted the manager's reasoning and suggestion that he purchase the replacements, which his insurance would pay for, and send them on the next shipment to Haifa.

Shortly after the big shipment to the Holy Land, Curtis received a letter from the Guardian instructing him to close the checking account. Curtis checked his records and discovered there was only three cents left. That amazed Curtis because although he was fastidious about keeping up-to-date and accurate records, he didn't send the Guardian a monthly statement. The bank sent all statements to Curtis.

In the letter he sent to the Guardian, stating that he had carried out his wish, Curtis included a three-cent postage stamp, which would balance out the account.

Curtis and Harriet's contribution to the Faith didn't go unnoticed by the Guardian. In a letter of June 6, 1949, Shoghi Effendi shared his feelings about the couple with them:

Dear and Valued Co-Workers:
Your constant services, rendered with such loyalty, zeal and perseverance, will never be forgotten, and are highly meritorious in the sight of God.

Be assured, happy and grateful and persevere in your noble endeavors. I will continue to supplicate on your behalf that the Master's richest blessings may crown your efforts with signal success.

Your true and grateful brother,
Shoghi

Ever since Curtis had returned from Haifa in 1922, he thought of when and how he would return. There was no question in his mind that he would revisit the place where part of him would always be. Even during the bleak days of the Great Depression, when he was hard-pressed to keep his family from being devoured by poverty, Curtis never gave up hope of walking on Mount Carmel again. Thirty years after his departure from Haifa, the way seemed clear for him to return, but this time with Harriet. A few good business years made it possible for him to go. So they applied for pilgrimage. A date was set, but about a month before they were to leave, the Guardian asked them to postpone the pilgrimage. Certainly Curtis and Harriet were disappointed, but they were sure there was a good reason for the Guardian's decision.

Though Curtis tried to be detached, an undercurrent of anxiety made him a little uneasy. Every phone-ring was expected to be notification of the new pilgrimage date. He anticipated the same thing from every letter from the National Spiritual Assembly or Haifa.

What Curtis sought finally came. For him the pilgrimage was also a reunion; and, in a sense, it was the same for Harriet, because of her relationship to Curtis over the years. His experiences with the Master had been ingrained into his being. There were times when she would look at him and feel the Holy Land.

The superficial differences in the Holy Land were startling to Curtis. Flying into a modern airport was a lot different from arriving at a primitive railroad station; in the drive from the airport to Haifa, Curtis marveled at the land-reclamation effort on the part of the Israelis, the new highways and buildings. And Haifa was no longer a sleepy little town steeped in ancient ways. It was a giant shipping port, with the Shrine of the Báb, standing majestically in the heart of Mount Carmel as a symbol of light and hope to the thousands of refugees from every part of the world who came by ship to resettle in the 'Promised Land.'

Curtis remembered the Shrine when it was a gray, one-story stone building that looked like a fort from the seashore. The beauty of the white and golden-domed 'Queen of Carmel' was greater when viewed in real life than in slides or snapshots back in America. As Curtis gazed at the Shrine, the thought of 'Abdu'l-Bahá came to mind and His efforts to erect at least the heart of the building that would hold the remains of the Báb, and to generate the momentum that would lead to its completion. Curtis knew how important the

Shrine was to the Master. 'Abdu'l-Bahá, he thought, must be happy.

To Curtis, Shoghi Effendi had changed considerably. He moved and talked like the Master. Following him on a walk on Mount Carmel, Curtis noticed Shoghi Effendi's shoulders fell the way the Master's did. In his presence, he felt some of the power that radiated from 'Abdu'l-Bahá. There was no doubt in Curtis' mind that God walked closely with Shoghi Effendi. One thing hadn't changed, and that was the gleam in Shoghi Effendi's eyes, that unmistakable sign of purity.

For Harriet, Curtis' presence provided an extra dimension to her pilgrimage, because he could point out what things were like in the time of the Master, and could feel His spirit. It was like being on two separate pilgrimages.

Like his mother, Curtis felt that Haifa was his real home. The pressures of business, the pettiness, the conniving, the backbiting, the negativity, the cynicism, the sarcasm that he encountered almost every day in America were happily missing from his life while on pilgrimage, as they had been thirty years back. The thought of returning after nine days disturbed him somewhat, but he realized that much Bahá'í work was needed in America, not only sharing the Bahá'í Message with people, but helping to strengthen existing Bahá'í communities. His head knew that, but his heart felt something else – he wanted to stay forever where the Master dwelt.

About midway through the pilgrimage, the Guardian asked Curtis and Harriet to stay about three more weeks. He needed Curtis to coordinate the installation of a water pump in Bahjí. Of course, they would stay, Curtis said. The decision didn't take much thought or time to make. Curtis was ecstatic, back in his work clothes, being where he dreamt of being and doing what the Guardian needed done. Somehow, working for the Faith in the Holy Land was the true fulfillment of his thirty-year-old feeling that one day he would be back in Haifa.

The twenty-six days Curtis and Harriet spent at the World Center were a journey through the Abhá Kingdom. Eating and chatting with Shoghi Effendi and discussing the progress of his work with him was reminiscent of the similar experiences Curtis had had with 'Abdu'l-Bahá. But there was a difference. With the Guardian there was more emphasis on the expansion of the Faith and the development of the Administrative Order. Curtis could sense as the Guardian spoke that he was witnessing a Divine General commenting on the unfoldment of a grand global campaign. With the Master, Curtis remembered individual spiritual development being stressed more.

To Harriet, one of the highlights of her stay in the Holy Land occurred one evening at the dinner table, when the Guardian looked at her and said, 'You and Curtis should be proud of the fact that all of your children are Bahá'ís; that had not even happened to the Holy Family.' Harriet viewed that as the supreme compliment; Curtis was moved also, but he always felt his children would embrace the Faith.

Curtis' faith was oak-firm. When the Guardian suddenly passed away in 1957, many believers teetered spiritually. 'How could there not be another Guardian?' some asked themselves, and in public. Curtis never wavered. He was a tower of strength that others leaned on, and from that association gained courage and understanding. A few days after the news of Shoghi Effendi's passing, Curtis contacted his children, who were all married at the time, assuring them that the present crisis would pass and pointing out that the believers in the past were confronted with similar storms and the Faith not only survived but grew in strength. He quoted from Bahá'u'lláh: 'He doeth whatsoever He willeth.'

Curtis took the passing of the Guardian as a personal loss, because he loved him so as an individual. But as in the time when he saw 'Abdu'l-Bahá's body stretched out on His bed, His spirit in the Abhá Kingdom, he couldn't weep. He felt that his helping to meet the goals of the Ten Year Crusade would make Shoghi Effendi a lot happier than spending days in solitude shedding tears.

Chapter 14

Though Curtis often talked about his experiences with
'Abdu'l-Bahá, he wasn't a nostalgic person. He was
forward-thinking, usually talking about the things he wanted
to do, his teaching plans, the places he wanted to visit and the
future of the Faith. Looking back at his life when he reached
seventy, he marveled at the speed of its unfoldment. You
could sense he could live many more lives in this plane of
existence, because he had so much mental energy, so many
ideas. He was a dreamer who enjoyed the challenge of
turning an idea into fact. Retirement was not for him,
because he never believed he was old. Oh, he knew his hair
had turned white, and there were more wrinkles on his face
than when he was thirty-five, and he was plagued by an
aneurysm which flared up whenever he pushed himself too
hard. But whenever pain shot across his side and he lay down,
you sensed he was saying to himself, 'Why does this dumb
thing have to happen to me? I have so many things I've got to
do.' It was a classic case of his vigorous soul being impatient
with his worn body. He couldn't wait until the pain subsided
so he could continue with his projects.

Curtis' enthusiasm never waned, even after suffering a heart attack in his new home in Bradenton, Florida. He never joined the shuffleboard and sun-tanning crowd. Besides teaching the Faith and being an active Auxiliary Board Member, he managed a local brokerage firm and sold mutual funds. A favorite expression of his was, 'It's better to wear out than to rust out.' And he would usually follow that statement with one of 'Abdu'l-Bahá's expressions: 'This life is a workshop, not an art gallery.' Curtis personified those expressions. He worked every day, especially for the Faith. Spending time at a mountain resort hotel, lounging around a pool or playing dominoes with a few cronies was something he wouldn't do. Vacations? He never really took what you would consider a conventional holiday. There were times when he would visit some Bahá'í friends in the Laurentian mountains in Canada, but in between motorboat rides he would conduct a deepening class or speak at a quickly arranged fireside. His greatest joy was going on teaching and deepening trips to summer schools, winter schools, special institutes in the north, south, east and west of the country. He rarely turned down an invitation from the believers, even in the last five years of his life when his heart condition worsened.

Even in his seventies, Curtis was putting about 40,000 miles a year on his Buick. In fact, his two longest teaching trips took place in the last two years of his life. Alaska and Hawaii beckoned. Fortunately, they were too far away to drive, although he was fascinated by the prospect of driving through the Canadian Rockies and Yukon to get to Alaska. He finally chose to fly, thanks to the insistence of Harriet. As for the Hawaiian trip, his doctor tried to discourage him from going, because he was beginning to have fainting spells. At times, when not enough blood reached his brain he would keel over. The friends in northern New Jersey remember that happening while he was at the Evergreen Cabin in Teaneck several months before his Hawaiian tour. Many in the audience felt that he had passed on, but a physician in the audience felt a heart beat. The friends carried him to a couch, where he was stretched out, his face almost chalk white. Healing prayers were recited. A few minutes later he sat up, making light of the incident. Actually, passing away at the Evergreen Cabin would have suited Curtis, because of what that building and grounds meant to him. He worked hard and long to make that property what it is now. A large Swiss-Chalet-like log cabin sits on about two acres of land, which include a pine grove and a carefully manicured lawn and rock garden in the heart of a residential section of Teaneck. It has become one of the sites to see in that town. During the late 1930s, 1940s and early 1950s Curtis spent many a free day helping to expand and beautify the place that his friend Roy Wilhelm had bequeathed to the Faith. Roy's large stucco house, where 'Abdu'l-Bahá spent several days in 1912, is in the grounds. The bedroom where 'Abdu'l-Bahá stayed has been set aside as a special place for people to visit. Curtis wired the cabin for electricity and helped build an extension and put together the rock garden. Many of the supplies he paid for.

For many years Curtis served on the national Bahá'í committee that oversaw the maintenance of the Wilhelm property. He was so close to the Evergreen Cabin, as it was called, that many of the friends considered him a fixture of the place. For some, coming there and not seeing him made the visit incomplete. He was usually there on Sundays for the weekly deepening that attracted people from different parts of metropolitan New York City. Many of his study classes were held there. The Teaneck Assembly, of which he was a member for many years, met there. Feasts were held there. The National Audio-Visual Aid Committee, which he helped to establish with Dr David Ruhe, Burt Dezendorf and Donald Kinney, had its headquarters at the Cabin. His children attended Bahá'í classes there for years. And there was his participation in the annual Souvenir, which was always a high point of the year for Curtis. The Souvenir is the gathering of hundreds of Bahá'ís and their friends to commemorate the Master's first Unity Feast in America, which was held on the Cabin grounds, the last Saturday of June in 1912. To prepare for this big event, he would spend many hours helping to groom the grounds and the interior of the Cabin. He enjoyed doing it, for it was like doing it for 'Abdu'l-Bahá. The Souvenir, he felt, was a time when the friends could feel the spirit of the Master. It was as if he sensed 'Abdu'l-Bahá walking among the picnicking people, showering cheer and love upon them.

The Master's association with the Cabin property, more than anything else, inspired Curtis to contribute so much of his time, energy and money to its development. In a sense, his working there was an extension of what he did in Haifa and Bahjí.

Before going to Alaska and Hawaii, Curtis went on a trip he thought would never materialize. It was the 1968 Oceanic Conference in Sicily and a three-day sojourn in the Holy Land. The idea of being back in Haifa and Bahjí, especially at his age – seventy-four – excited him. It wasn't his shaky health which would prevent him from going, because the prospect of passing away where the Master dwelt was an inducement to go. Mustering enough money to make the trip was the problem. When Emma Rice, an old friend of the Kelseys, heard of Curtis' desire to go, she insisted that he take a loan from her. Harriet, who decided to stay home, urged Curtis to accept Emma's offer and make the trip. She knew how much another trip to the Holy Land would mean to him; and she encouraged him to go, even though she realized there was a good chance that after seeing him off at the airport, she would never see him again.

Curtis, his old friend from New Jersey, Gus Wilcox, and Emma Rice went as a threesome to the conference, staying at the same hotel about twenty miles from the conference site. But the twenty miles seemed like 200 miles to Emma, because to get to the hotel, you had to pass a range of mountains. There were no expressways covering the distance as a crow flies. Instead, you had to drive on narrow roads that twisted around craggy mountains. To make matters worse, there were no guard rails. Emma knew what it was like to negotiate those roads, because she pioneered in Sicily for nearly ten years; and whenever she drove, she was careful to proceed cautiously. But driving with Curtis was a roller coaster experience. She remembered the transformation that took place in Curtis when he got behind the wheel of her rented car. He seemed like a youth longing for adventure. Evidently she wasn't aware of his reputation as an automobile speedster. Among the Bahá'í youth of the eastern United States, Curtis was known as 'the Bahá'í bullet.' Curtis roared along the mountain roads, at times screeching around sharp bends. After a while, Emma simply closed her eyes and prayed.

He did the driving in Israel, too, squeezing that in between the special pilgrimage tour. Curtis drove to the places where he had worked in 1921, showing Emma what he had done on Mount Carmel. As he began to explain how things like the lighting plant operated, his enthusiasm grew, very much like a boy showing off the best airplane model he had ever built. The fact that what he had done so long ago was still working pleased him. There was a gleam in his eye. In a way, Curtis was back in time, forty-seven years in the past, an eager lanky lad from the West thrilled to be doing what meant so much to the Master. His state of euphoria remained as he walked where he had walked with 'Abdu'l-Bahá and sat where he had sat with the Master in silence watching the sunrise, visited where he had gathered with others to hear 'Abdu'l-Bahá talk about the sacrifices made by the Persian friends and the unique mission the believers had. Watching Curtis relive what was the most memorable period of his life warmed Emma's heart; and she knew it wasn't easy for him to take her on his tour of the past, for he was in almost constant pain from a swollen artery inside his abdomen. Curtis knew he would never return to Haifa and Bahjí again, and leaving there was difficult. How fortunate, he thought, Hand of the Cause Mr Samandarí was, for he had passed away in the Holy Land during that special pilgrimage of 1968.

When Curtis returned to the United States, he didn't go on a rest and relaxation retreat. It was back to his Auxiliary Board work – and teaching. The trip to Alaska was invigorating. The people there reminded him of the people of the west when he was a youngster, men and women who took a sincere interest in a stranger and tried to make him comfortable. He found the Bahá'ís eager to learn more about their Faith and eager to share their Faith with others. His stories about his experiences with 'Abdu'l-Bahá and his insights into the Covenant thrilled the believers. He had transported them to a time and place they had read about. With Curtis, they were looking into the eyes that had gazed at 'Abdu'l-Bahá – and they sensed that Curtis had gained something special from his relationship with the Master. Alaska was Curtis' kind of country; he fitted neatly into the life-style. Pomp and pretense were as foreign to him as to the average Alaskan. And they sensed that he was like them, someone with a pioneering spirit, who enjoyed working and getting things done, who wouldn't think twice about rolling up his sleeves to chop down a tree if it had to come down. The Alaskan believers hated to see him leave and made him promise to return.

Before going to Hawaii, Curtis was deeply involved in organizing what he called the Florida Love Feast. Something like that was necessary, he felt, because so many of the friends didn't know each other, especially those who lived in different sections of the state. If the friends were more unified, he felt, the growth of the Faith in Florida would quicken.

He envisioned a weekend conference, with Hands of the Cause there, entertainment with Dizzy Gillespie, Seals and Crofts, and his daughter Carol, who was a professional singer. The conference was planned for February. But the most immediate project at. hand was his teaching and deepening tour of the Hawaiian Islands.

Curtis didn't go directly to Hawaii. Word reached some of the friends in California that he was on his way to Honolulu, and they urged him to spend several days with them, holding deepening classes, and possibly firesides. So he left Florida earlier than he had originally planned and spent several days on the west coast enchanting the friends with his experiences with the Master. His talks on 'Immortality and Eternality,' one of his favorite topics, enlightened many of those who came to hear him speak. Even people who were timid about the subject found Curtis' presentation refreshing. Curtis had success speaking on a subject that is often associated with grief and morbidity, because he made so much sense, and wove humour into what he had to say. It was also easy to notice that he believed absolutely in what he was talking about. In fact, his conviction was so strong that sensitive souls felt that he had a special periscope into the world after this life. Because he heeded the Master's exhortation to think about the next world as well as this one, Curtis not only prepared himself for the transition from this plane of existence to the next, but in some respects he was in tune with the extraphenomenal world. No, he didn't make an effort to delve into that world – just thought and meditated on it. Because he believed it was real, he was receptive to any messages from it. And they usually came in the form of dreams or premonitions. For example, his sister Kathleen, who died an hour after birth, and whom he often prayed for, came to him in a very vivid dream many years after her passing, mature and radiant, assuring him of her happiness. He awoke certain that he had met his sister.

Serving the Faith in Hawaii was a glorious experience from the start. About fifty believers were on hand to greet Curtis at the Honolulu airport armed with garlands of flowers, the traditional native symbol of warm welcome. The seven-hour flight was hard on Curtis, but as the garlands were placed around his neck, his spirit soared. How he wanted to share his Bahá'í experiences with these beautiful people, he thought. From that point on Curtis was radiant, enthusiastic and completely giving of himself throughout his stay. Only one or two people knew of his ailment.

Wherever he spoke, he drew large numbers of Bahá'ís. After all, the Bahá'ís of the island had not met many people who had lived and worked with 'Abdu'l-Bahá! His talks lasted longer than he planned, because the believers were fascinated by his stories about the Master, and how Curtis became a Bahá'í. Strange, but Curtis seemed to have the stamina to spend three hours speaking to the friends and answering their questions. It seemed that whenever he had to talk about the Faith a spurt of extra energy roared through him and he would be as animated and eager as a healthy youth. The Bahá'ís didn't view Curtis as an old, ailing man. They responded to his buoyant spirit and zest for life. Some followed him around, from meeting to meeting, often ending up in the same restaurants, usually Chinese eating-places, because Curtis loved Chinese food. For Curtis, Honolulu was an ideal place to be, because it probably had more Chinese restaurants than the state of Florida. Even his meals turned out to be deepening sessions with eager, wide-eyed youth.

For about two weeks Curtis moved from meeting to meeting at a whirlwind pace, taking time out to visit Hand of the Cause Agnes Alexander, who was living in a nursing home, and Martha Root's grave. But the highlight of his trip was his involvement in the Hawaiian Youth Conference. The young men and women seemed transfixed listening to him speak. He was so easy to relate to. Certainly he was no pompous character, no preacher, and not the faintest hint of condescension emanated from him. The youths' reaction to him was understandable, because through him they found themselves in the Master's house, sitting at His table, walking up Mount Carmel with Him; and what they had read about 'Abdu'l-Bahá came alive. They didn't want him to stop talking.

Why was Curtis so successful with young people? It was more than his sincerity and purity. Curtis never forgot what it was like being young. He was a kid at heart, and his young audiences sensed that; he was one of them.

When Curtis stepped off the airplane in Tampa, Florida, Harriet knew he was ailing. He looked so drawn. Even his smile and tan couldn't mask his weariness and pain. It wouldn't be long before he departed for the next realm, she thought.

But Curtis wasn't ready to go, at least not before organizing his next project – the Florida Love Feast. As soon as he got home he resumed putting together the project, which meant securing a place that could seat more than 500 people, working out the program format, developing materials to publicize the weekend conference which was less than two months away. As he worked, the pain in his side intensified. It got so bad that he spent most of the time in bed next to the phone, with a pad and pen. It was so important that every Bahá'í in Florida be at this conference that he tried hard to notify everyone about it and urged them to attend. For years he had dreamt of such a conference being held, for he felt it would be something 'Abdu'l-Bahá would want done. His commitment to the Master drove him, despite his illness, to realize that dream.

They came to the conference in Bradenton, Florida, from

every section of the state, even believers who hadn't been very involved in Bahá'í activity in recent years. In a way, it was an outpouring never experienced by most Florida Bahá'ís. Hands of the Cause John Robarts and William Sears came; so did Auxiliary Board Member William Tucker. And more than 500 believers, old and young, black and white, poor and rich, came to contribute to the joyous, heart-stirring affair where people felt free to shed tears of happiness and embrace each other wholeheartedly. It truly was a love feast.

Curtis was too ill to attend any of the sessions. Most of the time he was in bed; but people would come to him with reports as to what had happened. Hands of the Cause John Robarts and William Sears came to his bedside to share with him the spirit which he had worked so hard to generate at the conference. What he heard from Mr Robarts and Mr Sears cheered his failing heart. A smile of contentment crossed his tired face whenever someone reported what had happened at the conference. His joy was not prompted by a feeling of achievement; but because 'Abdu'l-Bahá would approve of what was happening at the love feast.

Hand of the Cause William Sears sensed the special spirit at the event: '... The conference created a feeling of precious closeness to our beloved Master, 'Abdu'l-Bahá. Throughout his long years of service to our cherished Cause, Curtis has always brought us especially close to 'Abdu'l-Bahá. It seemed as though the Master were there at each session to fulfil every hope that Curtis had, and to see the glorious fruition of all his plans.'

A few days after the conference, Curtis was rushed to the hospital. The swollen artery inside his abdomen had enlarged, and there was the danger of its bursting any moment, killing him. Emergency surgery was needed.

Curtis survived the surgery; but he was placed in the intensive care unit, because there was no assurance that what was done would hold. A day and a half after the operation, on February 20, 1970, Curtis passed away, a few weeks from his seventy-sixth birthday. It happened, Curtis most likely would say, because 'God doeth whatsoever He willeth.'

Curtis never wanted people to fuss over his passing. Why waste so much energy and money over a corpse when the reality of the human being has passed on and is functioning? 'Bury me in a simple wooden box, without any monument,' he would say. Harriet carried out his wish, interring his body in a cemetery in St Petersburg, Florida. Harriet, Emma Rice and daughter Carol accompanied the casket to the grave site, which had a simple plaque at its head. On it Harriet had inscribed what she felt best characterized her husband: 'He loved and served 'Abdu'l-Bahá.'